William Blake

The Tyger

Edited by
Winston Weathers
The University of Tulsa

The Merrill Literary
Casebook Series
Edward P.J. Corbett, Editor

Charles E. Merrill Publishing Company
A Bell & Howell Company
Columbus, Ohio

Standard Book Number   675-09443-7

Library of Congress Catalog Number: 72-84930

1 2 3 4 5 6 7 8 9 10 – 73 72 71 70 69

Printed in the United States of America

Foreword

The Charles E. Merrill Literary Casebook Series deals with short literary works, arbitrarily defined here as "works which can be easily read in a single sitting." Accordingly, the series will concentrate on poems, short stories, brief dramas, and literary essays. These casebooks are designed to be used in literature courses or in practical criticism courses where the instructor wants to expose his students to an extensive and intensive study of a single, short work or in composition courses where the instructor wants to expose his students to the discipline of writing a research paper on a literary text.

All of the casebooks in the series follow this format: (1) foreword; (2) general instructions for the writing of a research paper; (3) the editor's Introduction; (4) the text of the literary work; (5) a number of critical articles on the literary work; (6) suggested topics for short papers on the literary work; (7) suggested topics for long (10-15 pages) papers on the literary work; (8) a selective bibliography of additional readings on the literary work. Some of the casebooks, especially those dealing with poetry, may carry an additional section, which contains such features as variant versions of the work, a closely related literary work, comments by the author and his contemporaries on the work.

So that students might simulate first-hand research in library copies of books and bound periodicals, each of the critical articles carries full bibliographical information at the bottom of the first page of the article, and the text of the article carries the actual page-numbers of the original source. A notation like /131/ after a word in the text indicates that *after* that word in the original source the article went over to page 131. All of the text between that number and the next number, /132/, can be taken as occurring on page 131 of the original source.

Edward P.J. Corbett
General Editor

General Instructions
For A Research Paper

If your instructor gives you any specific directions about the format of your research paper that differ from the directions given here, you are, of course, to follow his directions. Otherwise, you can observe these directions with the confidence that they represent fairly standard conventions.

A research paper represents a student's synthesis of his reading in a number of primary and secondary works, with an indication, in footnotes, of the source of quotations used in the paper or of facts cited in paraphrased material. A *primary* source is the text of a work as it issued from the pen of the author or some document contemporary with the work. The following, for instance, would be considered primary sources: a manuscript copy of the work; first editions of the work and any subsequent editions authorized by the writer; a modern scholarly edition of the text; an author's comment about his work in letters, memoirs, diaries, journals, or periodicals; published comments on the work by the author's contemporaries. A *secondary* source would be any interpretation, explication, or evaluation of the work printed, usually several years after the author's death, in critical articles and books, in literary histories, and in biographies of the author. In this casebook, the text of the work, any variant versions of it, any commentary on the work by the author himself or his contemporaries may be considered as primary sources; the editor's Introduction, the articles from journals, and the excerpts from books are to be considered secondary sources. The paper that you eventually write will become a secondary source.

Plagiarism

The cardinal sin in the academic community is plagiarism. The rankest form of plagiarism is the verbatim reproduction of someone else's words without any indication that the passage is a quotation. A lesser but still serious form of plagiarism is to report, in your own words, the fruits of someone else's research without acknowledging the source of your information or interpretation.

You can take this as an inflexible rule: every verbatim quotation in your paper must be either enclosed in quotation marks or single-spaced and inset from the left-hand margin and must be followed by a footnote number. Students who merely change a few words or phrases in a quotation and present the passage as their own work are still guilty of plagiarism. Passages of genuine paraphrase must be footnoted too if the information or idea or interpretation contained in the paraphrase cannot be presumed to be known by ordinary educated people or at least by readers who would be interested in the subject you are writing about.

The penalties for plagiarism are usually very severe. Don't run the risk of a failing grade on the paper or even of a failing grade in the course.

Lead-Ins

Provide a lead-in for all quotations. Failure to do so results in a serious breakdown in coherence. The lead-in should at least name the person who is being quoted. The ideal lead-in, however, is one that not only names the person but indicates the pertinence of the quotation.

Examples:

(typical lead-in for a single-spaced, inset quotation)

```
Irving Babbitt makes this observation about
Flaubert's attitude toward women:
```

(typical lead-in for quotation worked into the frame of one's sentence)

```
Thus the poet sets out to show how the present
age, as George Anderson puts it, "negates the
values of the earlier revolution."⁷
```

Full Names

The first time you mention anyone in a paper give the full name of the person. Subsequently you may refer to him by his last name.

Examples: First allusion—Ronald S. Crane
```
            Subsequent allusions—Professor Crane,
            as Crane says.
```

Ellipses

Lacunae in a direct quotation are indicated with *three spaced periods,* in addition to whatever punctuation mark was in the text at the point where you truncated the quotation. *Hit the space-bar of your typewriter between each period.* Usually there is no need to put the ellipsis-periods at the beginning or the end of a quotation.

Example: "The poets were not striving to communicate with their audience; . . . By and large, the Romantics were seeking . . . to express their unique personalities."[8]

Brackets

Brackets are used to enclose any material interpolated into a direct quotation. The abbreviation *sic,* enclosed in brackets, indicates that the error of spelling, grammar, or fact in a direct quotation has been copied as it was in the source being quoted. If your typewriter does not have special keys for brackets, draw the brackets neatly with a pen.

Examples: "He [Theodore Baum] maintained that Confucianism [the primary element in Chinese philosophy] aimed at teaching each individual to accept his lot in life."[12]

"Paul Revear [sic] made his historic ride on April 18, 1875 [sic]."[15]

Summary Footnote

A footnote number at the end of a sentence which is not enclosed in quotation marks indicates that only *that* sentence is being documented in the footnote. If you want to indicate that the footnote documents more than one sentence, put a footnote number at the end of the *first* sentence of the paraphrased passage and use some formula like this in the footnote:

[16] For the information presented in this and the following paragraph, I am indebted to Marvin Magalaner, Time of Apprenticeship: the Fiction of Young James Joyce (London, 1959), pp. 81-93.

Citing the Edition

The edition of the author's work being used in a paper should always be cited in the first footnote that documents a quotation from that work. You can obviate the need for subsequent footnotes to that edition by using some formula like this:

⁴ Nathaniel Hawthorne, "Young Goodman Brown," as printed in <u>Young Goodman Brown</u>, ed. Thomas E. Connolly, Charles E. Merrill Literary Casebooks (Columbus, Ohio, 1968), pp. 3-15. This edition will be used throughout the paper, and hereafter all quotations from this book will be documented with a page-number in parentheses at the end of the quotation.

Notetaking

Although all the material you use in your paper may be contained in this casebook, you will find it easier to organize your paper if you work from notes written on 3 x 5 or 4 x 6 cards. Besides, you should get practice in the kind of notetaking you will have to do for other term-papers, when you will have to work from books and articles in, or on loan from, the library.

An ideal note is a self-contained note—one which has all the information you would need if you used anything from that note in your paper. A note will be self-contained if it carries the following information:

(1) The information or quotation *accurately* copied.
(2) Some system for distinguishing direct quotation from paraphrase.
(3) All the bibliographical information necessary for documenting that note—full name of the author, title, volume number (if any), place of publication, publisher, publication date, page numbers.
(4) If a question covered more than one page in the source, the note-card should indicate which part of the quotation occurred on one page and which part occurred on the next page. The easiest way to do this is to put the next page number in parentheses after the last word on one page and before the first word on the next page.

In short, your note should be so complete that you would never have to go back to the original source to gather any piece of information about that note.

Footnote Forms

The footnote forms used here follow the conventions set forth in the *MLA Style Sheet*, Revised Edition, ed. William Riley Parker, which is now used by more than 100 journals and more than thirty university presses in the United States. Copies of this pamphlet can be purchased for fifty cents from your university bookstore or from the Modern Language Association, 62 Fifth Avenue, New York, N.Y. 10011. If your teacher or your institution prescribes a modified form of this footnoting system, you should, of course, follow that system.

A primary footnote, the form used the first time a source is cited, supplies four pieces of information: (1) author's name, (2) title of the source, (3) publication information, (4) specific location in the source of the information or quotation. A secondary footnote is the shorthand form of documentation after the source has been cited in full the first time.

Your instructor may permit you to put all your footnotes on separate pages at the end of your paper. But he may want to give you practice in putting footnotes at the bottom of the page. Whether the footnotes are put at the end of the paper or at the bottom of the page, they should observe this format of spacing: (1) the first line of each footnote should be indented, usually the same number of spaces as your paragraph indentations; (2) all subsequent lines of the footnote should start at the lefthand margin; (3) there should be single-spacing within each footnote and double-spacing between each footnote.

Example:

[10] Ruth Wallerstein, Richard Crashaw: A Study in Style and Poetic Development, University of Wisconsin Studies in Language and Literature, No. 37 (Madison, 1935), p. 52.

Primary Footnotes

(The form to be used the *first* time a work is cited)

[1] Paull F. Baum, Ten Studies in the Poetry of Matthew Arnold (Durham, N.C., 1958), p. 37.

(book by a single author; p. is the abbreviation of *page*)

[2] René Wellek and Austin Warren, Theory of Literature (New York, 1949), pp. 106-7.

(book by two authors; pp. is the abbreviation of *pages*)

[3] William Hickling Prescott, <u>History</u> <u>of</u> <u>the</u> <u>Reign</u> <u>of</u> <u>Philip</u> <u>the</u> <u>Second,</u> <u>King</u> <u>of</u> <u>Spain,</u> ed. John Foster Kirk (Philadelphia, 1871), II, 47.

(an edited work of more than one volume; *ed.* is the abbreviation for "edited by"; note that whenever a volume number is cited, the abbreviation p. or pp. is *not* used in front of the page number)

[4] John Pick, ed., <u>The</u> <u>Windhover</u> (Columbus, Ohio 1968), p. 4.

(form for quotation from an editor's Introduction—as, for instance, in this casebook series; here *ed.* is the abbreviation for "editor")

[5] A.S.P. Woodhouse, "Nature and Grace in <u>The</u> <u>Faerie</u> <u>Queen</u>," in <u>Elizabethan</u> <u>Poetry</u>: <u>Modern</u> <u>Essays</u> <u>in</u> <u>Criticism</u>, ed. Paul J. Alpers (New York, 1967), pp. 346-7.

      (chapter or article from an edited collection)

[6] Morton D. Paley, "Tyger of Wrath," <u>PMLA</u>, LXXXI (December, 1966), 544.

(an article from a periodical; note that because the volume number is cited no p. or pp. precedes the page number; the titles of periodicals are often abbreviated in footnotes but are spelled out in the Bibliography; here, for instance, *PMLA* is the abbreviation for *Publications of the Modern Language Association*)

Secondary Footnotes

(Abbreviated footnote forms to be used after a work has been cited once in full)

[7] Baum, p. 45.

(abbreviated form for work cited in footnote #1; note that the secondary footnote is indented the same number of spaces as the first line of primary footnotes)

[8] Wellek and Warren, pp. 239-40.

     (abbreviated form for work cited in footnote #2)

[9] Prescott, II, 239.

(abbreviated form for work cited in footnote #3; because this is a multi-volume work, the volume number must be given in addition to the page number)

[10] <u>Ibid</u>., p. 245.

(refers to the immediately preceding footnote—that is, to page 245 in the second volume of Prescott's history; *ibid.* is the abbreviation of the Latin adverb *ibidem* meaning "in the same place"; note that this abbreviation is italicized or underlined and that it is followed by a period, because it is an abbreviation)

[11] Ibid., III, 103.

(refers to the immediately preceding footnote—that is, to Prescott's work again; there must be added to *ibid.* only what changes from the preceding footnote; here the volume and page changed; note that there is no p. before 103, because a volume number was cited)

[12] Baum, pp. 47-50.

(refers to the same work cited in footnote #7 and ultimately to the work cited in full in footnote #1)

[13] Paley, p. 547.

(refers to the article cited in footnote #6)

[14] Rebecca P. Parkin, "Mythopoeic Activity in the Rape of the Lock," ELH, XXI (March, 1954), 32.

(since this article from the *Journal of English Literary History* has not been previously cited in full, it must be given in full here)

[15] Ibid., pp. 33-4.

(refers to Parkin's article in the immediately preceding footnote)

Bibliography Forms

Note carefully the differences in bibliography forms from footnote forms: (1) the last name of the author is given first, since bibliography items are arranged alphabetically according to the surname of the author (in the case of two or more authors of a work, only the name of the first author is reversed) ; (2) the first line of each bibliography item starts at the lefthand margin; subsequent lines are indented; (3) periods are used instead of commas, and parentheses do not enclose publication information; (4) the publisher is given in addition to the place of publication; (5) the first and last pages of articles and chapters are given; (6) most of the abbreviations used in footnotes are avoided in the Bibliography.

The items are arranged here alphabetically as they would appear in the Bibliography of your paper.

Baum, Paull F. Ten Studies in the Poetry of Matthew Arnold. Durham, N.C.: University of North Carolina Press, 1958.

Paley, Morton D. "Tyger of Wrath," Publications of
    the Modern Language Association, LXXXI (Decem-
    ber, 1966), 540-51.

Parkin, Rebecca P. "Mythopoeic Activity in the Rape
    of the Lock," Journal of English Literary
    History, XXI (March, 1954), 30-8.

Pick, John, editor. The Windhover. Columbus, Ohio:
    Charles E. Merrill Publishing Company, 1968.

Prescott, William Hickling. History of the Reign of
    Philip the Second, King of Spain. Edited by
    John Foster Kirk. 3 volumes. Philadelphia: J.B.
    Lippincott and Company, 1871.

Wellek, René and Austin Warren. Theory of Litera-
    ture. New York: Harcourt, Brace & World, Inc.,
    1949.

Woodhouse, A.S.P. "Nature and Grace in The Faerie
    Queene," in Elizabethan Poetry: Modern Essays in
    Criticism. Edited by Paul J. Alpers. New York:
    Oxford University Press, 1967, pp. 345-79.

*If the form for some work that you are using in your paper is not given
in these samples of footnote and bibliography entries, ask your instructor for advice as to the proper form.*

Contents

Introduction	1
A Facsimile	6
The Tyger by William Blake	7
S. Foster Damon, *The Tyger*	8
Roy P. Basler, *"The Tyger": A Psychological Interpretation*	12
Jesse Bier, *A Study of Blake's "The Tyger"*	15
Stanley Gardner, *The Tyger*	26
Martin K. Nurmi, *Blake's Revisions of* The Tyger	34
Hazard Adams, *"The Tyger" as an Example*	52
E. D. Hirsch, Jr., *The Tyger*	67
Philip Hobsbaum, *A Rhetorical Question Answered: Blake's Tyger and Its Critics*	74
Morton D. Paley, *Tyger of Wrath*	80
Rodney M. Baine, *Blake's "Tyger": The Nature of the Beast*	104
Kay Parkhurst Long, *William Blake and the Smiling Tyger*	115
Suggestions for Papers	122
Additional Readings	125

Introduction

William Blake, born November 22, 1757, lived his sixty-nine and three-quarter years in England during a period of economic, political, and cultural revolution. In many ways his life, which ended August 10, 1827, can be viewed as a consistent, continuing reaction to the rage and torrent of his times. Yet, just as reasonably, Blake can be seen as a man splendidly removed from the topical and the local altogether, a man who lived in a world of his own creation, beyond history, in the kingdom of his imagination.

Indeed, the modern reader must acknowledge and accept two seemingly different William Blakes. One Blake was the provincial but liberal Englishman, sympathetic with revolution and reform, concerned with the improvement of the social order and the abolishing of its economically-rooted evils, critical of out-dated institutions and mores, and eager for the recognition and success of his own humanistic values in a vulgar, noisy, cruel world. The other Blake was the Bible-reading mystic, conversing and dining with the scriptural prophets and saints, refusing to compromise his faith and vision in any way, drawing portraits of dead and ancient heroes, creating his own literary mythology in order to present his apocalyptic vision: a man proudly alienated from a great deal of the important secular action of the day.

Blake, even in his own lifetime, was a paradox. Some of his enemies thought him hopelessly mad, some of his disciples thought him a saint. Both his sweetness and irascibility were well known. He was, and is, an enigma. Yet no one can deny his magnificent creative gift—and no one can step into the unique world of his creation without emerging a richer and more sophisticated person. In psychedelic jargon, Blake brought his own thing onto the scene: he made it really happen. More and more twentieth-century readers are making contact with his mind and his experience.

1

Blake was born and reared in London at 28 Broad Street (now Broadwick Street), a few blocks from Golden Square in the Carnaby Market district. As a boy he was perceptive and imaginative, and so frequently reported the amazing things he had seen—God jumping up at the window; angels in a tree on Peckham Rye—that even his hosier-merchant father thought it best that Blake not suffer the rigors of formal schooling. Instead he allowed him to go to Henry Pars' drawing school (1767) and five years later to be apprenticed to James Basire, the engraver (1772). Blake spent an intense and rewarding six years of study with Basire, and after his apprenticeship he studied briefly at the Royal Academy. In 1782, he married Catherine Boucher, an illiterate girl from Battersea, south of the Thames, set up his own household, and made his living by engraving illustrations for various publishers. For a brief time he entered into a partnership with James Parker and opened a print shop, but Blake was not a successful merchant and had to rely finally upon his own handicraft.

For the first years of his adult life, William Blake seemed destined for moderate success as a free-lance engraver; but he was, without question, in an uncertain business, and he and Catherine, moving from one residence to another in London, felt more and more the precarious position of the artist in late eighteenth-century London—especially an artist more adventurous and more original than established orthodoxies could finally tolerate. What pleased Blake did not always please his customers.

In 1800, Blake accepted an offer to move from London to the village of Felpham in Sussex, on the ocean's edge—to serve as something like private artist and engraver for William Hayley, a gentleman poet and scholar. Blake and Catherine lived at Felpham for three years, but by the end of that time Blake, feeling he was too much under Hayley's thumb, and that his creative genius was being reduced to mediocrity, returned to London, where he remained for the rest of his life. It was at Felpham, however, that he gathered his philosophical strength, conceiving the shape and dimension of the great works he was later to produce; and it was also at Felpham that he had the quaint experience of being accused of treason by a soldier who had trespassed in Blake's Felpham garden. As a result of the accusation, Blake had to go to court where he was easily acquitted; yet it was an experience that was to confirm for Blake the suspicions he had always had of all earthly governments and institutions, and the realization he had of the evil and fallen nature of secular man.

Back in London, Blake found life increasingly difficult: he received fewer commissions, he was sinking deeper into obscurity, and he and his wife were reduced to poverty. They were increasingly dependent upon the charity of a few loyal friends and admirers. In these years, early in the nineteenth century, Blake had hope that through his own publications—the illuminated books that he wrote, drew, colored, printed, bound himself—he might find some success and reward, but such was not to be the case. Those economically bleak years may, however, have been Blake's greatest so far as the history of English literature is concerned for it was in these years, even as his health broke, that he produced his two final masterpieces, *Milton* and *Jerusalem*.

Late in his life, Blake's reputation increased, and he acquired some enthusiastic young disciples who called themselves the Ancients. With their aid, especially with the aid of John Linnell, the Blakes were able to eke out a tolerable existence, producing the illuminated books that Catherine now helped put together and color. Blake took on major new assignments such as the illustrations for Dante's *Divine Comedy*, uncompleted illustrations on which he was working the last year of his life.

Amazingly enough, Blake was scarcely known as a poet in his lifetime, though he had been a writer nearly all his days, beginning to put his words down on paper as early as his twelfth year. Only one book of his was published in the conventional way: *The Poetical Sketches*, a collection of Blake's juvenilia, which his temporary friends, the Mathews, and his artist friend Flaxman financed. One other work, the first book of his *French Revolution* (supposedly to have twelve books when finished), got as far as galley proofs, but Johnson, the bookseller, who had planned to publish the work, never completed the project. All the remaining poems that Blake made public were "published" by Blake himself, not set in type, but engraved and illustrated the special way that Blake developed which remains uniquely his own. The first of these illuminated works was *Songs of Innocence*, produced in 1789, to be followed by *The Book of Thel* in the same year. Other great illuminated books by Blake are *The Marriage of Heaven and Hell* (c. 1790-93), *Visions of the Daughters of Albion* (1793), *America* (1793), *Europe* (1794), *Urizen* (1794), *The Song of Los* (1795), and *The Four Zoas* (1797), all climaxed by the production of *Milton* (1808) and *Jerusalem* (1818).

No quick or easy summary can be made of Blake's writings. Yet certain general observations can be stated. In all his work, Blake maintained, by and large, a critical—often hostile—attitude toward a rational, highly-organized, institutional, restrictive way of life that he believed was the product of the scientific method and the rationalism of such men as Francis Bacon, John Locke, and Isaac Newton. And in all his work, he advocated and praised an imaginative, human, creative, energetic sort of existence in which our true humanity can most meaningfully exert itself, and which can result, for the individual or for the state of mankind as a whole, in a new Jerusalem that is literally a transformation of our understanding and vision of the universe in which we live. Blake's work is, quite frankly, evangelistic, propagandistic, and militant in a most excitingly esthetic way, and he created—in order to articulate his philosophy of transformation—a new mythology, in which *Ulro* becomes the name of our fallen, upside-down world; *Eternity* becomes the name of the true and proper state of existence; *Christ* becomes representative of the Great Compassionate Humanity Divine, the godhead to which individuals may aspire and which is the personification of a divine grace operative in the universe; *Urizen* becomes the name of the man-made Jehovah-like rational god that circumscribes, dogmatizes, and moralizes human existence into its fallen and perverted condition; and *Los* becomes the name of man's imaginative and creative potential.

Obviously, Blake presents certain difficulties to his readers. Many of his poems demand repeated and thoughtful readings before they come into perfect focus—and some, even after a close and careful study, remain lost in dark shadows so far as meaning and message are concerned. Even when Blake's poems are obscure, however, they are moving and beautiful experiences. Blake, after all, is one of the great lyric voices of English poetry, and once we have read his unique and provocative lines, we never forget them. No other poet speaks in quite the same way, and no other music sounds quite the same.

Perhaps Blake's most famous single poem is "The Tyger," a fairly short poem that he included in *Songs of Experience* in 1794. Blake had earlier written *Songs of Innocence* (1789), and then five years later he added the experiential melodies in order to show, he said, "the Two Contrary States of the Human Soul." "The Tyger" has something to do, obviously, with the life of "experience" as differentiated from the life of "innocence," but its exact and final meaning may never be determined—for, obviously again, its meaning depends a great deal upon how any individual reader responds to the ideas of innocence and experience and evaluates the particular terms Blake used in the poem.

On one level, "The Tyger" is a fairly simple poem; it does not contain—as some of his later poems do—references to his difficult and private mythology. Yet "The Tyger," on another level, is a stimulating and beautiful riddle, a simply-stated enigma, that means various things to various people—as the essays that follow in this casebook amply reveal.

A study of "The Tyger" is the best possible introduction to Blake's philosophy and art. Wrestling with the problems of "The Tyger," we bathe in the magic of Blake's creativity. Trying to answer the questions that

Blake presents in "The Tyger," we find ourselves upon the threshold of new intellectual perspectives and new intellectual adventures. And that is what Blake's art and poetry are all about. Blake's great life-long quest was to bring himself and his fellowmen to a radical new vision of reality; to ponder the "eternal questions" and to break through all limitations, not to specific answers to the questions but to a whole new realization of what the questions mean. Blake wanted to discover the meaning of human experience in the eternal scheme of things. He devoted his art and poetry to a fiery, imaginative discussion of man in the eternal drama that takes place in the theater of infinity. "The Tyger" is a brief but compelling example of Blake's achievement.

* William Blake's "The Tyger" from *Songs of Innocence and of Experience*, Orion Press with Trianon Press. Reprinted by permission.

The Tyger

Tyger, Tyger, burning bright,
In the forests of the night:
What immortal hand or eye
Could frame thy fearful symmetry?

In what distant deeps or skies
Burnt the fire of thine eyes?
On what wings dare he aspire?
What the hand dare seize the fire?

And what shoulder and what art
Could twist the sinews of thy heart?
And when thy heart began to beat,
What dread hand? and what dread feet?

What the hammer? what the chain?
In what furnace was thy brain?
What the anvil? what dread grasp
Dare its deadly terrors clasp?

When the stars threw down their spears
And water'd heaven with their tears:
Did he smile his work to see?
Did he who made the Lamb make thee?

Tyger, Tyger, burning bright,
In the forests of the night:
What immortal hand or eye
Dare frame thy fearful symmetry?

7

S. Foster Damon

The Tyger*

This poem is undoubtedly the best known of all Blake's works, and one of the very great poems in the English language. Every school child knows it, and yet its thought is so profound that it touches everywhere upon the problems of all thinkers. Even in Blake's own day, when most of his poems were quite unknown, this one was circulated everywhere, for it was unforgettable. It was the first thing that Lamb ever heard of Blake's: 'I have heard of his poems, but have never seen them. There is one to a tiger...which is glorious!' [1] Lamb used to misquote this poem with much fervour. Such circulation always causes variants; and when the authentic text was published, protests appeared in various magazines, giving the lines 'to which we are accustomed.'

Out of the great paragraphs of praise which have been offered up to this poem, we can pick two or three notes of dislike. Rossetti thought the poem so imperfect that when he reprinted it he practically rewrote it. I am glad to record that his emendations have never been accepted. Cestre, looking for madness, found its beginning here: 'Blake a perdu sa serenite. A partir de ce moment, son esprit se trouble. Il ne conserve assez de lucidite pour concevoir un plan de poème intelligible.'† We could as easily accuse Cestre of madness for being unable to perceive the perfectly obvious development in the poem. Mr. Percy Cross Standing, in an article entitled *Was Blake a Poet? (The Catholic World*, July 1905), called this poem 'arrant drivel!'

---

* Reprinted from *William Blake: His Philosophy and Symbols* (Boston: Houghton Mifflin Company, 1924), pp. 276-278. Reprinted by permission of Houghton Mifflin Company, Boston, and Constable and Company, Ltd., London.

[1] Gilchrist, ch. xiii. [Alexander Gilchrist, *The Life of William Blake*. London, 1957.]

† ["Blake has lost his equanimity of mind. And henceforth, his soul is troubled. He does not maintain enough intellectual lucidity to organize an intelligible poem." Charles Cestre, *La Revolution Francoise et les Poetes Anglais*, p. 215. Paris, 1906.]

The Tyger deals with the immense problem of Evil. It is the same problem which Musset expressed so excellently in his *Espoir en Dieu*: /277/

> Comment, sous la sainte lumière,
> Voit-on des actes si hideux,
> Qu'ils font expirer la priere
> Sur les lèvres du malheureux?
>
> Pourquoi, dans ton oeuvre céleste,
> Tant d'éléments si peu d'accord?
> A quoi bon le crime et la peste?
> O Dieu juste! pourquoi la mort?*

Blake could not consider Evil abstractedly. His God was essentially personal: therefore Evil must be his Wrath. 'God out of Christ is a consuming fire,' he wrote elsewhere;[2] and Crabb Robinson recorded that Blake said of Christ, 'He is the only God.'

The problem of The Tyger is, quite simply, how to reconcile the Forgiveness of Sins (the Lamb) with the Punishment of Sins (the Tyger). So it is evident that the climax of *The Tyger*: Did he who made the Lamb make thee?' is not an exclamation of wonder, but a very real question, whose answer Blake was not sure of. The 27th *Proverb of Hell* distinctly states that 'The roaring of lions, the howling of wolves, the raging of the stormy sea, and the destructive sword are portions of eternity too great for the eye of man.'

Nevertheless Blake found some good in Wrath. 'The wrath of the Lion is the Wisdom of God,' and 'The Tygers of wrath are wiser than the Horses of instruction,' are two other *Proverbs of Hell*. In Iamblicus's *Life of Pythagoras*, he may have come across the sentence: 'It is necessary to purify the woods, in which these passions have fixed their abode, with fire.' Certainly in his Paracelsus he found much praise of wrath:

---

* ["How is it that under the light of heaven,
  One can see acts and events so hideous
  That they kill any sort of prayer
  Upon the lips of an unfortunate viewer?

  "Why, in your heavenly work and doing,
  Are there so many elements in discord?
  For what possible reason do crime and disease exist?
  O just God! Why is there such a thing as death?" Ed.]

[2] On a painting in the Tate Gallery. I have not been able to trace the history of this phrase. It used to be much quoted by Calvinists as a proof of the reality of Hell; but it is not to be found in the Bible, as they supposed.

Destruction perfects that which is good; for the good cannot appear on account of that which conceals it ... By the element of fire all that is imperfect is destroyed or taken away (*Preface* to the *Coelum Philosophorum*).

Fire separates that which is constant or fixed from that which is fugitive or volatile (*De Morbis Metallicis*, Lib. II. Tract 1).

The three prime substances are proved only by fire, which manifests them pure, naked, clear, and simple. In the absence of all ordeal by fire, there is no proving of a substance possible. For fire tests everything, and when the impure matter is separated the three pure substances are displayed (*De Origine Morborum*, Lib. I. cap. 1).

Fire is the father or active principle of separation (Third of the *Fragmenta Medica*).

A digression must be made here on the universal use of fire as a symbol of wrath. Blake, as we have seen, used it in his sentence, 'God out of Christ is a consuming fire'; and in *Urizen* he speaks of 'Flames of eternal fury.' Böhme, in his fourth Epistle (103), wrote of 'the mystery of the wrath, or fire of God's anger.' In the *Faerie Queene* (II. iv. xxxv.2) Spenser wrote: 'Wrath is a fire.' Milton also spoke of 'flames, the sign of wrath awaked' (*Paradise Lost*, VI. 58). Blake's association of fire with his Tyger (ll. 1,6,8) was due to the old symbol.

Another very old symbol is that of the Forest. The Forest, in Blake, is the world of Experience, where the many sterile errors (dead trees) conceal the path and dim the light. Dante, on his way to Hell, was lost in this identical forest (*Inferno*, I. ll. 1-9). Thomas Vaughan ('Eugenius Philalethes') also began his greatest work, the *Lumen de Lumine*, by losing himself in a forest at night. Shelley's *Epipsychidion*) contains several references to this forest: 'the wintry forest of our life ... struggling through its error ... the obscure Forest ... that wintry /278/ wilderness of thorns ... the grey earth and branches bare and dead.' Blake was very fond of the symbol. It occurs on the title-page of *The Marriage of Heaven and Hell*, in the margin to the 9th illustration of *Job*, and many other places. It is blown flat in the 6th plate of the *America* and the margin of the 13th illustration of *Job*.

With these two symbols fixed in our mind, we can see readily the answer to the question of the function of Wrath, concealed in the very first lines of the poem:

> Tyger, tyger, burning bright
> In the forests of the night.

Blake intends to suggest that the great purpose of Wrath is to consume Error, to annihilate those stubborn beliefs which cannot be removed by the tame 'horses of instruction.'

But this does not explain whence Wrath came. Blake asks the question characteristically. 'What immortal hand or eye'—that is, what mechanistic force of nature, or what glance of divine vision—dared this creation? The answer is concealed in the poem. I have already explained the meaning of stars to Blake—that they represented an inferior order of the created world, which is ruled by Reason, or Urizen. In the later books, Blake often depicted Urizen as weeping over the anguish which he has caused, and even terrified at it. Remembering this, we can readily understand the lines:

> When the stars threw down their spears,
> And water'd heaven with their tears.

The Tyger was created in this fallen world of Reason, produced by its mechanical laws; and his appearance caused Urizen's Aristotelean reactions of terror and pity. The exact moment of his creation is described in *The Four Zoas*, VIII. 439. Reason (Urizen), caught in the clutches of Dogmatic Morality (Rahab), has sunk below even a semblance of human form into that of a dragon (warfare—the 'struggle for life'). It is then that all the beasts appear, as Swedenborg taught, and Urizen in despair realizes that he has fallen to yet a lower plane in his struggle for dominion. But the end of all this evil is nearly at hand. Revolt (Orc) breaks loose, and the Last Judgment hangs over Creation.

The order of the lyric is typical of Blake. He shows the entire process of the tyger's creation. First the 'fire of his eyes' is gathered from the cosmos; then the heart is created, the feet forged, and ultimately the brain. This is not unlike the creation of Urizen himself, as described in *Urizen, The Book of Los,* and *Milton* (5:9-27). Blake probably began the tyger with the creation of his eyes, because the Eye to Blake meant Intellect, as opposed to the Wing of Love. Blake describes the creation by a series of white-hot exclamations rather than by an elaborate description. The effect is one of an intense improvisation; but an examination of the manuscript shows at once that Blake made a great many corrections *during* the composition of the first draft.

Roy P. Basler

The Tyger:
A Psychological Interpretation*

Those readers who have studied this poem in academic environment know that a certain meaning has been attached to it. I merely ask that they withhold that meaning for the moment and examine the poem afresh. For any who have not /21/ received this traditional interpretation through instruction, no impediment need be set aside.

Consider the image presented in the first stanza, and the question asked. What is the simplest communication made by the image? Terror in the beholder, power to harm in the image. Beyond this there is communication of something not wholly of this world. Tigers do not burn, though the color of the tiger may suggest fire; jungle forests may be so dark as to suggest night, but could not be with strict rational logic called "forests of the night." What we have in the image is of the mind surely, but not of the rational conscious mind wholly. It is something of a dream image, conveying terror before a symbol of power to harm, and, like all dream images, made of the stuff known to the conscious mind but given in a fusion of non-sequiturs (fire-tiger-forest-night) which have nevertheless linking associations and analogies: tigers roam the forests, and darkness and fire (light) are archetypal opposites in any language or experience. The communication of fear before power to harm lies in what the poet and reader see as a mental image.

Continuing with the question asked in the first stanza, we find a query which supposes that the image has been created, "framed" by a hand, instructed by an eye, even as a painter paints a picture, and that the creator is perhaps immortal (not of this world) and the image awe-inspiring in symmetry (perfection). But the query is not a statement, please note. As a question it asks rather than answers "Whence came this image?" We shall

* Reprinted from *Sex, Symbolism and Psychology in Literature* (New Brunswick: Rutgers University Press, 1948), pp. 20-24, by permission of the author.

keep this in mind to apply to the other questions asked in following stanzas, for the poet is not necessarily positing anything beyond the images.

The questions which continue in the rest of the poem reiterate and elaborate the question of the first stanza, the elabo- /22/ ration suggesting the possibility of an other-worldly or non-natural creator. Not until the next-to-last stanza, however, is there any specific, undebatable reference to deity. There, in an allusion to the unsuccessful revolt of the angels which provides *Paradise Lost* with its antecedent action, the question is put: Did God smile at the victorious conclusion of the war in heaven and then create something more terrible than Satan's pride? The allusion to the lamb provides an obvious contrast with the tiger, but also introduces a possible clue to allegory, since the lamb is the traditional symbol of peace and Christ-like spirit. Biblical reference to the lion and the lamb as symbols of extremes in nature comes to mind at once, and the reader may leap to an interpretation of the tiger as the Anti-christ, except that such an interpretation would be anticlimactic when the poet employs "dare" to replace "could" in repeating the first stanza as the poem's conclusion. There would be little daring involved for a supreme God who has smiled at the victorious conclusion of one struggle if he created nothing more terrible than the satanic power he had already vanquished. Surely the tiger does not represent Satan, but something more terrible, whether or not created by God. But perhaps the question is not meant by the poet to imply an affirmative answer, and we may do well to reconsider.

Upon reflection, the tiger may not represent the supernatural at all, but something within the soul of man. Blake's poetry testifies abundantly to the fact that he was most appalled by the infinite extremes of the human psyche, love-hate, trust-fear. Psychologically this symbolism has little that can be objected to. It provides a satisfactory symbolic climax in the poem's conclusion to match the dramatic climax of the rhetorical questions reached in the reference to deity in the next-to-last stanza, and, what is more significant, provides a /23/ powerful meaning which turns on the new word "dare" which replaces the "could" used in the first stanza. The question at last is: Would an immortal deity dare create on earth something more fearful than the power he had thrown out of heaven? The question is left to the reader for answer.

This seems to me the most satisfactory reading of the poem. The traditional interpretation that the tiger symbolizes the "Wrath of God" does not make sense to me now and did not when I first read the poem years ago, although I had then no alternative. It fails to make sense, not because the tiger is inapropos as a symbol of divine wrath, but because the dramatic framework includes deity as a possible creator of the tiger, not as the tiger itself. The poet's inclusive question is: What creator can be conceived capable of perpetrating man's scope for fear and hate?

The psychological implications of the poem are satisfying whether one answers the poet's question with God as creator, or with life-force as creator. From a Freudian point of view, the psyche encompasses the extremes symbolized in tiger and lamb no less than does the mythology which Blake created in his poetry. The orthodox Christian mythology does not encompass both extremes in deity, but does in man. The relegation of Satan to a secondary power, permitted to pursue evil by an absolute God who is thus responsible for the continuation of what He could at any moment terminate, is an anomaly which theology has rationalized but has never made wholly acceptable to human intelligence.

Hence Blake's question in this poem, like his questions in other poems, was meant in the eighteenth century to challenge orthodox theology and at the same time the too simply rational deism which was in intellectual favor at the time. Both deism and orthodox Christianity failed Blake, apparently, because /24/ they divorced the dual aspects of the soul on a supernatural plane, and deism failed even further by its impossible attempt to dismiss the darker aspect from this world by insisting that since a reasonable deity created it, "Whatever is, is right." Blake understood in his fashion, no less than Freud, the duality ruling the realm of the psyche.

Jesse Bier

A Study of Blake's "The Tyger"*

The rare talent of William Blake (1757-1827) expressed itself in a variety of forms, especially in painting, engraving, and poetry. His reputation as an English poet has been a changing one, for Blake has been difficult to place neatly in any of the standard categories of literary history and criticism. Blake's independence of spirit and uniqueness as an artist may be explained in part, then, as an outgrowth of a quite liberally endowed genius. His individualism can be seen, too, as a reflection of a period: the age in which he lived was one of wide, popular self-assertion, to which human impulse the political and social revolutions of America and France bear witness. His most famous works, in whith "The Lamb" and "The Tyger" are central symbols, parallel through no mere coincidence the dates of the French Revolution. The collection, "Songs of Innocence," appeared in 1789, and the succeeding group of poems, "Songs of Experience," came out in 1794. "The Tyger," a poem in the latter collection, is the finest single demonstration of William Blake's deeply stimulating achievement in the realm of English poetry. I place it at the outset, opposite its counterpart in "Songs of Innocence," as an aid to the reader and as an introduction to this study.

The Lamb

(From "Songs of Innocence")

Little Lamb, who made thee?
  Dost thou know who made thee?
Gave thee life, and bid thee feed
By the stream and o'er the mead;

The Tyger

(From "Songs of Experience")

Tyger! Tyger! burning bright
In the forests of the night,
What immortal hand or eye
Could frame thy fearful symmetry?

---

* Reprinted from *Bucknell University Studies*, I (June, 1949), 35-46, by permission of the publisher and the author.

Gave thee clothing of delight,
Softest clothing, woolly, bright;
Gave thee such a tender voice,
Making all the vales rejoice?
  Little Lamb, who made thee?
  Dost thou know who made thee?
  Little Lamb, I'll tell thee,
  Little Lamb, I'll tell thee:
He is called by thy name,
For he calls himself a Lamb.
He is meek, and he is mild;
He became a little child.
I a child, and thou a lamb,
We are callèd by his name.
  Little Lamb, God bless thee!
  Little Lamb, God bless thee!

In what distant deeps or skies
Burnt the fire of thine eyes?
On what wings dare he aspire?
What the hand dare seize the fire?   /36/

And what shoulder, and what art,
Could twist the sinews of thy heart?
And when thy heart began to beat,
What dread hand? and what dread feet?

What the hammer? what the chain?
In what furnace was thy brain?
What the anvil? what dread grasp
Dare its deadly terrors clasp?

When the stars threw down their spears,
And water'd heaven with their tears,
Did he smile his work to see?
Did he who made the Lamb make thee?

Tyger! Tyger! burning bright
In the forests of the night,
What immortal hand or eye
Dare frame thy fearful symmetry?

"The Tyger" is a short poetic masterpiece that best demonstrates a whole quality of mind—philosophic, mystic, intuitive, visionary—and a poetic diction representative of a poet whose position in English literature becomes increasingly eminent and consolidated as the years pass by and literary criticism grows more attentive to the work of that poor man but rich genius. As a poem in itself, "The Tyger" begins to take on infinitely more meaning than it has had as a simple but imaginative child's poem, standing in contrast to the much more easily understood poem in "Songs of Innocence." It begins to be seen as an achievement vastly more subtle and suggestive than first impression might imply. It reveals a technique that is a clear example of conscious art, a process of composition that informs every line and every word. It points up a poetic talent unique for its creative method, profound for its felicitous approach to and intimacy with the symbols of thought and insight. In an era when a great deal of modern poetry is very much concerned with the treatment of symbols and the effects of intensity of feeling, often harking back to Donnean metaphysics for suggestions of approach and expression, it is not amiss to re-appraise this significant poem of Blake's from these points of view, to study him more deliberately and closely. In a time, too, when American critics and

the American public begin to pay the belated attention due to Herman
Melville, it may prove stimulating and provocative of further investigation
to compare the whale in Melville's masterpiece of myth and symbolism
with Blake's baffling but alluring "Tyger." /37/

The first paradox of Blake is that he is identified with the beginnings of
the romantic age in English poetry (a blazing link between the
pre-Romantic-Thomson-through-Burns-school and the great poets to come
in the full Romantic period), but that, like John Donne one hundred and
fifty years or so before him, he is one of those poets beyond
categorization: not only a departure from the period before neo-classicism.
but so unique a reaction to it that he is in his own class. He is, then, at
once the first clear signal of romanticism, yet also such a grand variation
on that new strain that he, like Shakespeare, is an exclusive literary figure.

Blake can be better appreciated, however, if we briefly consider him in
comparison with Donne, no small literary variation himself. Both reacted or
revolted against the poetic tradition immediately preceding their careers:
Donne against the weakened lyric tradition, Blake against the satiric style
that was current and the confinement and triteness of expression and
thought that heroic couplet had come to impose on poetic genius. Both
men, then, were stylistic rebels, speaking out as individuals. Yet they
differed, too, in approach and basic conception: where Donne sought
eloquence through the theology and formalized faith of his day, Blake saw
no indebtedness to institutions, and this lack of connection permitted him
to make the most unpredictable of poetic flights. Both men are very close
in a quality of genuine intensity characteristic of their temperaments,
poetic and personal, but there is a gulf as wide as the universe between the
intellectual efforts of the first and the spiritual voyages of the second. One
dealt with conceits in order to wring out the paradoxes of reason in his
work, twisting his language to follow the convolutions and contours of his
deep and provocative thoughts. The second chose to deal in symbols in
order to flash the intimations of his spirit and the consciousness of his
soul, impossible to express conventionally, upon the surface of language;
we shall see that his problem, though as profound as Donne's, was yet
more difficult in the elusiveness of the issue, and, perhaps, in the
fundamental contradiction between human (or social) communication and
that personal inner experience which is inaccessible, formless, and
unspeakable. But side by side with the powerful but incommunicable
experience in Blake was the equally persuasive and insurgent impulse to
reveal his vision somehow, and the world has it in the mystic, striking,
originally con- /38/ notative and supremely imaginative and lyric poems of
this poet, who breathed and dreamed in a tremendous and exciting universe
of paradox and ultimate Nirvana.

Blake's art is three-fold, consisting of poetry, painting, and music.[1] "The Tyger," as an example, is certainly poetry. It is painting in the visual evocation of the lines, and music in the sound and swing of the words and lines. Let us consider the content of "The Tyger" now, and then journey on to whatever philosophical or artistic realms the discussion will take us.

Why does Blake choose the "tiger" as his title and central symbol? Surely, the poem in "Songs of Experience" is a counterpart of "The Lamb" in "Songs of Innocence." Is not the opposite of the lamb the lion? Before we even begin an analysis of the stanzas, we must settle the image, first of the lamb, secondly of the lion, thirdly of the tiger. If the conclusion is to be, after all, superficial, we may deepen comprehension later without becoming inconsistent.

"The Lamb" represents a fairly understandable image.

> Little Lamb, who made thee? . . .
> Little Lamb, I'll tell thee:
> He is callèd by thy name,
> For he calls himself a lamb.

This is a clear reference to the use of this word in John and in Revelation.[2] The word is a diminutive that expresses the endearing relation in which Jesus stands to us: He the "precious Lamb," we one with Him (and a union with God is also mentioned in Isaiah). This whole concept is summed up in the poem thus:

> He is meek and he is mild;
> He became a little child.
> I a child and thou a lamb.
> We are called by his name.

The obvious Biblical opposite to the lamb is the lion, a much more complex symbol, however. The "roaring lion," as well as the subtle serpent, is Satan in I Peter. In the Old Testament, Messiah is the Lion of the Tribe of Judah, yet—and here we pause and hold the philosophical issue open—it is also the Lamb, combining opposites. That Blake uses the lion-symbol in its simpler form (as /39/ evil) and in its more abstruse context (wrath and innocence indissolubly mixed) is evident in at least two other poems. In "Night" from "Songs of Innocence" we have:

---

1 William Butler Yeats, *Poems of William Blake* (London, 1893), p. xvii.

2 Andrew Robert Fausset, *Bible Cyclopedia* (London and New York, n. d.), p. 420.

that do not concern us here—his exquisite workmanship for all the gods, with additional associations around him of anvil and hammer. He is, in fact, the "god of skill and fire,"[5] the god of the plastic arts, and—in a significant way for us—he is invariably pictured with his hammer and his chiton, a type of dress that, pointedly here, leaves his whole shoulder free to work. The symbol of the Creator is thus an amalgamated one. Certainly, we do not censure Blake for his multiple allusions. In a way, too, we need *not* know that the figure of Creator here is more than one mythological character, but knowing it, we can appreciate the quick, simultaneous, developing allusions that are solidifying and rushing to culminate in the climax of the next stanza.

Fourth stanza

What the hammer? what the chain? (What were the tools?)
In what furnace was thy brain? (In what beaker was your essence?)
What the anvil? what dread grasp
Dare its deadly terrors clasp? (What god could wield these tools and hold,
  let alone make—for it is made now—the power and terror you are?)

The symbol of the Creator is complete here. He is Prometheus in his "forethought," Vulcan in his identity with fire, Hephaestus as the supremely skilled smith of the universe, and even Thor, for that god's hammer and anvil and frequent identification with Jove. In total, he is the creator, skillful beyond comparison, daring in plan, omnipotent for the task. And the tiger that has emerged? Its strength (of heart) can only be imagined by the force of its creation, a force that could and dared to "twist" (and the word becomes superhuman) its sinews. It, itself, is force and power, "deadly" and terrible. It is cruelty, and it is that baffling malign thing that stands contrary, if not antithetic, to the lamb. Why, at this point, the "tiger" can be called this is a question answered by Blake in another poem, "The Divine Image," ending "Songs of Experience," which has direct pertinence to the middle passages just concluded. /42/

> The Human Dress is forged Iron
> The Human Form a fiery forge,
> The Human Face a Furnace sealed

a poem, too, that names the cruel, jealous, terrible, secret, and hungry side of man, which is just as true a "divine image" as mercy, pity, peace, and love (in the previous "Divine Image" of "Song of Innocence") are characteristics of our lamb-like nature. We are now ready for a comment.

---

[5] William Smith, ed., *Dictionary of Greek and Roman Biography and Mythology* (Boston, 1849), II, 383.

Fifth stanza

When the stars threw down their spears,
And water'd heaven with their tears,
> (Lightning and thunderstorm—the actual, fulminatory
> beginning of the working universe)

Did he smile his work to see?
> (A smile for the inscrutable mystery he has produced in
> the world and in each soul)

Did he who made the Lamb make thee?
> (The previous simile suggests a positive answer to this
> question, and this problem of Creator and Meaning is
> answered thus by other works of Blake)

This climactic stanza, then, comments only in asking the great, fundamental question: is God one, and if He is, did He make two different things, and are these creations not at war with one another, and is the "tyger," then, a symbol of more than evil—of reconciliation, of union, of God (smiling), Himself? Its answer is a question, but the question, taken together with the unabhorrent tone of the whole poem, is an answer itself and is bolstered by what outside material, in Blake, we can further bring to bear on the philosophic matter.

The sixth stanza is a duplication of the first, save for one significantly altered word—"dare" has replaced "could" in the creative activity, and we have a concluding shift from a start that suggested caution and impossibility to a finish that states temerity and the *fait accompli*.

Does, then, the tiger represent for Blake what the whale, later in our country, may have meant for Melville: that wicked, galling impropriety of Creation, that wrathful half of the universe, that outward, powerful tormenting evil that frustrates man, and, just as validly, that inward perverse and masochistic animal that constitutes one half of each individual human soul? Blake's poem and his other work do equate the tiger with the later American symbol /43/ of *Moby Dick*, but because Blake is much farther along the mystic road, his tiger is a more suggestive image, too.

Let us define some larger terms for a moment, and orient ourselves. Let us look upon mysticism, for instance, as the art of establishing conscious relation with the Absolute.[6] But because Blake did not partake of any formalized or formularized mysticism, let us not mistake this mystical experience for a philosophy. Now what, however, is the Absolute? This, because Blake was an artist and *not* a philosopher, is not defined for us. It is not so much a state of spiritual rest as it is a kind of union of Indwelling Love and transcendent Light. It is more the latter for Blake, and the

---

6 Evelyn Underhill, *Mysticism*, Revised Edition (New York, 1930), p. 49.

symbolism he employs (not to describe a state of rest, but a higher plane of active being) is a symbolism that *travels*, showing the soul outward bound to its home. We are getting close to the core of Blake: he is for activism as opposed to passivity, prophetic vision as against static reason, the "tigers of wrath" as against the "horses of instruction." The mysticism of Blake is a vision: the vision of the prodigious and unthinkable metamorphosis of the human mind,[7] the identification of God and Man. Now this is, we see, an Oriental concept. Does the Far Eastern symbolism—"Yang and Yin," a very useful graphic representation of universal forces, by the way—help us here?

Yin, we find, is the negative force, imagined as dark clouds over the sun, as water, too. Yang, we discover, is the positive force, the unclouded sun-disc, seen often as fire (coincidence of coincidences!). Yin and Yang, like the tiger and the lamb, are abstract correlates,[8] each coming into existence at the other's expense (seasonal representations for the Chinese), hard and soft principles, motion and rest. Now, Nirvana is the equilibrium between Yin and Yang, and this balance, this state of psychic beatitude, implies an actuating force: an access of desire to generate blissful karma. It implies (to translate Toynbee for our particular use here) a challenge to which there can be a mystical response. Only, this mystical response on the part of Blake was his own, unfettered by philosophical school or theological sect: it was *Imagination* for him, and for Blake /44/ Imagination is identified with Fire. (This, of course, is his predominant symbol and image in "The Tyger." Also, the vision of a generated universe—even a re-generated one for Blake in some of his other poems—by some process of metal and fire is a central image for him in the "Four Zoas," where the symbolism is clearly that the furnace is our natural body, the bellows our lungs, and the hammer our heartbeat.[9] This last reinforces our interpretation of the third and fourth stanzas.)

The upshot of the Yin-Yang polarity is not actually antagonism, in the deep sense, but a rhythmic mutuality, an alternating ascendance and decline, an ultimate balance. No one force *wins*. There is only, in the last sense, no conquest or defeat, as such, but union. Fire isn't antithetical to water, if you will. It is *with* water a necessary part of our universe. Experience is not at variance with innocence; it is *contrary*, not contradictory, to it; it is, for instance, the doubt that reforms belief. The "tiger" is the flame of disbelief through which we must go, for instance, to

---

[7] Northrop Frye, *Fearful Symmetry* (Princeton, 1947), p. 70.

[8] Arnold J. Toynbee, *A Study of History*, Abridged Edition (New York and London, 1947), pp. 201-203.

[9] Northrop Frye, *op. cit.*, p. 253.

kill the fiction that man's desire is lawless and evil. In the profound sense, the "tiger" in our world must be the validation, on another plane, of the "lamb" in our world, experience the proof, on a newer level, of innocence. In the most personal sense, the "tiger" is, in fact, not sheer unadulterated evil and perversity in the outer world, but, like Moby Dick again, the face of creation, ever-ambiguous, the marvelous and the fatal together, within each of us.

For Blake, however, if not for Melville later, the creation of the "tiger" is a "smiling" creation, because the "dread" and "terrible" thing, "burning" there in the "forests" of our mundane world, is intimate with the Absolute itself, identified with it, present with it on earth. Indeed, that "essential thing" that the "tiger" is Blake portrays in a striking, beautiful context. His mysticism we can understand now, is different: he attempts the reconciliation of reality and the ideal on earth. His symbols for this effort are inimitable to begin with, shifting in actual use, elusive in conclusion, and fashioned out of the texture of Nature. He is, in effect, engaged in the colossal task (needing its own furnace and hammer) of translating the truth of his inner visionary world into the beauty of this one.[10] He struggles to disclose great matters by imperfect means, /45/ and his symbols, revoked so originally, so uniquely connotative, are suggestive of his own inner imaginative being, to the study of which an outsider must bend his complete, constant, sympathetic attention.

We should conclude this study with some remarks on poetic style in "The Tyger." An inventory of diction, for example reveals how many ways Blake varies his "fire" image: *burning, bright, burnt, fire* again twice, and *furnace.*

The second, third, and fourth stanzas are interesting illustrations of accelerated imagery: shorter lines, actually choppy in expression, help give the feeling of speed. The fifth stanza has significantly longer, more flowing lines, slowing the pace. On the one hand, rapidity is a stylistic aid to the dazzling picture of creation, and on the other, the slower pace helps give pause and weight to the completed activity. And the two variables, quickness and measure, are enclosed symmetrically (not fearfully) by almost identical stanzas.

The impatience we permitted Blake in his symbolic allusions to the Creator we allow him, too, in his language. The last line of the second stanza—

What the hand dare seize the fire?

---

[10] Evelyn Underhill, *op. cit.*, p. 274.

is not grammatical perfection, but he does not really need small verbals or pronouns if he does not want them. Things are going too fast and excitingly here for us to become picayune in our demands.

There are, too, some alliterative touches[11] in the poem, nailing the piece together: *burning bright, frame* and *fearful, distant deeps, shoulders* and *sinews,* and *art* and *heart* as approximate alliterations (as "eye" and "symmetry" are approximate rimes), *began* and *beat, stars* and *spears, smile* and *see,* and, of course, *Tiger, Tiger*—all of which are too close to one another to be accidental.

We recall, in viewing the poem as a synthetic whole now, rather than analyzing its constituent parts as we have been doing, that for Blake poetry, painting, and music were the three powers of art to which he paid homage. This is poetry in its miraculous blend of thought, feeling, and expression. The poem is music in its lyricism, a kind of sonata (*allegro* and *andante* with the theme at either end). /46/ It is painting in that it evokes brilliant, colorful, naturalistic images that flash upon the mind visually.

Here it is that we can remember, too, a biographical note—Blake's antagonism to the neo-classic art about him. And in this pervasive protest he made against the restrictions of his day—in all arts—we come back to his pioneering romanticism: his belief that the Absolute, at least, for him, is achieved through the Imagination, and his less profound but equally significant feelings about human fellowship, freedom, positivism. In the pre-romantic line (the Thomson-to-Burns school) he can be fitted as an expanding influence; in the romantic line (the Wordsworth-through-Byron school) he can be hailed as the initial exponent, for his opposition to restraint, denial, exploitation, convention. But, like Donne, whom he resembles in intensity, but differs from in approach and fundamental character, he is a variation too.

In the true sense, he is individual enough, great enough perhaps, to stand alone and apart from convenient categories. He is "bright" enough to burn all by himself in the "forests" of the literary "night."

A literary figure of these proportions (more timeless than "romantic"), with this proficiency in art, these characteristics of mind, these institutions of spirit, and these reconciliations of philosophic opposites, may have a good deal to say and suggest to a generation newly appreciative of the metaphysical technique of Donne, newly preoccupied with the profound symbolisms of Melville, and perennially haunted by the contradictions of its own time in thought and feeling.

---

11 Alfred Kazin, *The Portable Blake* (New York, 1946), p. xxiii.

Stanley Gardner

The Tyger*

The Tyger extends into realm beyond realm of meaning. The implications in those six short verses are more vast than in anything else Blake wrote of comparable length, and the concentration of cosmic distance and depth, within a single fiery frame, is intense. And, having caught infinity within two burning eyes, and eternal action in a single deed, Blake, in the incredible afterthought that now stands as the fifth stanza, gathers yet another universe of meaning to the immensity he has already grasped.

I use the word 'gathers' rather than 'adds' because the afterthought is completely assimilated into the meaning of the poem. It is no mere addition, as the rejected stanza would have been. Yet the relevance of the stanza of the Lamb has been challenged by critics. Such a challenge seems to me to be based on a failure to realize the poem as a whole. If the poem is fully realized as far as stanza five, that stanza comes as a breath-taking but inevitable extension of what the poet has already written, and its rightness is unquestionable.

At the beginning 'the glowing tyger' (cp. *Albion*, 1. 210, p. 200) burns in the 'forests of the night'. In the second stanza the fire of his eyes burns 'in distant deeps or skies'. The word 'burning', being repeated in 'Burnt', concentrates the whole being of the tyger in the *fire* of his eyes, a concentration reinforced in the question:

What immortal hand or *eye*?

which keeps the mind of the reader on this aspect of the creator, as well as of the tyger. The echo of 'burning' in 'Burnt' and the repetition of the

* Reprinted from *Infinity on the Anvil* (Oxford: Basil Blackwell, Publisher, 1954), pp. 123-130, by permission of the publisher.

26

fire symbol also carries the reader into an association of the 'forests of the night' with 'distant deeps or skies'. The fire of the tyger burnt in these realms—the 'vast forests' of Urizen 'shut in the deep' (cp. *Urizen*, i, 5). In *The Book of Urizen*, the book of Creation, Blake developed the symbol of the forest to infinite range, by exactly the same association of ideas as appears in *The* /124/ *Tyger*, a poem of creation. The implications of that infinite forest of darkness, and of the immense symbol of the ocean, are essentially relevant to *The Tyger*, and the importance of *The Book of Urizen* to the full realization of *The Tyger* needs to be stressed. The range implicit in the phrase 'distant deeps or skies' is self-evident. The imagination sweeps from the vast symbol of the spatial ocean, to the skies, a movement intensified by the related meaning in

> On what wings dare he aspire?
> What the hand dare seize the fire?

where the first line takes the imagination in an arc of flight from deep to sky, and the second sets the hand around the fire that burns there. The skies, moreover, are the skies of *night*—'the forests of the night'—a conception which leads to the *stars* of the 'Lamb' stanza, and provides a link of poetic meaning there, as will be seen.

'The tygers of wrath' are beasts of ferocious revolt in Blake, as well as animals of predatory instinct—lust—which stalk the Child and the Lamb of Innocence. Whichever meaning we associate with the tyger in this poem, it is clear that a symbolic connotation is intended. The tyger of revolt burns in the forests of oppression. A hand seizes this fire as the fire of revolt is seized in *A Song of Liberty*. Or the tyger is the burning ferocity of the lustful 'king of night', which is seized and fixed within the frame of mortality. Both meanings are acceptable, and both may be present. Not only is *The Book of Urizen* relevant to *The Tyger*, but *America* is too, where we see revolt generated from within the symbols of the forest and the deep.

No detail extraneous to the poetic meaning is given, either of the tyger or of the creator of the tyger. The first stanza sets the fire of the tyger in the eternal night, and suggests the power of the eye or hand that could contain its 'fearful symmetry' within a 'frame', within a physical body. We are not concerned with the *mind* of the creator anywhere in the poem. His is entirely an act of corporal strength, and our imagination is fixed on the limbs engaged. In the second stanza the relationship between the tyger and the eternal forest and ocean is extended, until the complementary theme is reasserted in the final question of the stanza:

> What the hand dare seize the fire?

Within the symbolic implications there is this juxtaposition of the timeless, immortal distances of forest, night, and deep, and the /125/ measured, mortal concentration of fixing the tyger's symmetry within a finite frame. Both themes are introduced in the first stanza, and repeated in stanza two, where the question 'On what wings dare he aspire?' forms the link between the two themes. The transition having been made, and the wrath of the tyger having been seized, the imagination is focused on the intensely corporal theme, on the shoulder which can 'twist the sinews' of the tyger's heart; and on the 'art' which directs the power of the shoulder. This word 'art' gives the action immensity, besides bringing abstract creative thought into synthesis with the intensely creative deed. 'Art' always implies two things in Blake: physical labour and length of time; that is precisely the two 'opposites' which are reconciled in this poem. Thus, when Urizen charges his 'Bow of the clouds of secrecy', he fixes 'The sinew in its rest', and lodges in it the Rock,

> plac'd with art, lifting difficult
> Its weighty bulk.
>
> (*Ahania*, ii, 7.)

Urizen describes elsewhere his gifts to mankind; 'jewels & precious ornament labour'd with art divine', and 'Sweet instruments of sound' 'invented with laborious art' (*The Four Zoas*, vi, p. 301). This connotation of 'art' is constant in Blake's writing. We are told in *The Four Zoas* how Eno 'took a Moment of Time And drew it out into seven thousand years with much care & affliction'; and that

> She also took an atom of space & open'd its centre
> Into Infinitude & ornamented it with wondrous art.
>
> (p. 257.)

In *Jerusalem* we learn how Los 'compell'd the invisible Spectre'

> To labours mighty with vast strength, with his mighty chains,
> In pulsations of time, & extensions of space like Urns of Beulah,
> With great labour upon his anvils, & in his ladles the Ore
> He lifted, pouring it into the clay ground prepar'd with art.
>
> (i, II.)

In these two quotations we see the word related to infinity, and to the forge symbol; these two dominant associations and that of art with incessant labour indicate the meaning of the word in *The Tyger*.

As the intensity of the physical action deepens, the tyger ceases to be a fire in the forests of eternity, and meets mortality. As soon /126/ as the sinews of the heart are knotted into existence they pulse with mortal life:

> And when thy heart began to beat
> What dread hand & what dread feet
>
> Could fetch it from the furnace deep
> And in thy horrid ribs dare steep
> In the well of sanguine woe?
> In what clay & in what mould
> Were thy eyes of fury roll'd?
>
>   (p. 87; 94.)

Thus Blake first trailed after the symbol of the furnace of Los, and the symbol of the human body as an abyss into which the heart was lowered. The 'furnace' in the rejected stanza has no relationship with its adjective 'deep'. Nor is the word 'deep' used here intended to carry any reference to the word 'deeps' used earlier in the poem. The association is false.

Moreover, we find, if we turn to *The Book of Urizen*, that, in the riveting of the changes of Urizen by Los the heart, while it sinks into the frame of mortality,

> Deep down into the Abyss,

and there begins to beat,

> Panting, Conglobing, Trembling
>   (iv [B], 7.)

—the heart is in no way associated with the forge of Los. Much less does the heart begin to beat *before* it comes out of this creative forge, as Blake states in the rejected stanza. In rejecting it Blake cancelled a passage in which the absolute truth of the symbolism is fractured. Whether or not the rejection was consciously reasoned, the result in the poem as it stands is a complete fusion of symbol with action, in which the symmetry of the symbolism is completely maintained.

The heart begins to beat, and the verse measures its beat with it. The word 'feet'—only a mere factual detail when the rejected passage followed it—has, in the final version, a poetic significance. Once it no longer leads into a straightforward sentence as the apparently irrelevant subject of the verb 'could fetch', we associate it strongly with its rhyme 'beat', and the association gives the word 'feet' its inherent movement. We are no longer aware of its choice for the sake of rhyme, for the rhyme becomes inseparable from the full poetic meaning. Further, the transition from the beginning of /127/ the heartbeat to the reference to the feet of the creator is true to reality. As the heartbeat gives the tyger life distinct from the creator, so the word 'feet' gives the creator corporal existence distinct from his act of creation. It *separates*.

This same sequence occurs in *The Book of Urizen*. Once the riveting of Urizen's changes is complete, and he first moves in temporality, we are told how he flung his arms wide,

> And his feet stamp'd the nether Abyss.
> (iv[B], 12.)

This is the function of the word in the third stanza, and it acquires its full meaning from the rejection of the stanza of false symbolism that originally followed it. The word also has a significance for the stanza that replaces the cancellation, the stanza that epitomizes the forge of Los. The question at the end of stanza three sets the feet firm, before the hammer is wielded in the 'dread hand'. The questions are so complete in their poetic sequence that grammar becomes pointless, and the reader's imagination leaps from the hand to the feet planted on the floor of the forge, and thence to the hammer swung in the hand. The sequence from the hammer to the chain and the furnace is equally inevitable; and the question 'What the anvil?' sends the imagination back to the stance suggested in the question 'and what dread feet?'

It has been shown how the synthesis of the heart with the furnace of Los in the rejected stanza was alien to Blake's symbolism. In its place Blake introduces the hammer, and the beaten chain, and the brain. Now while the heart was not put through the fire in *The Book of Urizen*, the brain *was*, and it was specifically related to all the symbols used in the final version of *The Tyger*: 'Forgetfulness, dumbness, necessity, In chains of the mind locked up,

> Los beat on his fetters of iron,
> And heated his furnaces, & pour'd
> Iron sodor and sodor of brass.
>
> Restless turn'd the Immortal inchain'd.
> (iv [B], 4–5.)

The chaining of the intellect is a symbolic action common throughout Blake, and in *The Tyger* it replaces a stanza that would have destroyed the poem's unity. The body, with its five finite senses, forged round the

infinite mind, separates that mind from its infinity; and once more we are
led to an inevitable poetic sequence, for the /128/ introduction of this new
intellectual relevance gives Blake the opportunity to return again from the
particular corporal deed to the spatial theme, and to ask of the tyger's
brain, as he did of 'the fire':

> what dread grasp
> Dare its deadly terrors clasp?

The imagination at once moves away from the location in the forge of
physical creation, and we associate this less specific question with the first
theme of the poem—the setting in the 'forests of the night' in space—since
it echoes the earlier transitional question:

> What the hand dare seize the fire?

It may be added that the presence of concrete detail in that question
(hand, fire, seize) leads *towards* the immediate concrete action, while the
abstracts in the later question (dread grasp, deadly terrors, and the static
verb, clasp) lead *away* from the physical act to a more spacious perspective.
The poetic control is complete.

Now, as we have seen, the one power that has dared to grasp the
'deadly terror' of the tyger in the night is Innocence; a and the next stanza
is the stanza of the Lamb. Blake has already led our imagination away
from the specific deed, towards the spatial theme, originally in preparation
for the concluding stanza:

> Tyger, Tyger, burning bright
> In the forests of the night.

But the preparation is as apposite to the 'stars' of the present fifth stanza
as it is for 'night', and the star symbol is closely related to the symbols of
the forest and the sea, as we have seen. Thus the new symbol of the stars
is in direct relationship with the initial spatial theme in all its aspects (the
forests, the deep, the skies, and the night, and even the fire). This is hardly
a mere addition that breaks the unity of the poem.

It is true that the poem would have had a more *obvious* unity had the
stanza of the Lamb been omitted. The mind had travelled from the black
forests of the night into the glowing forge of the creation, making a
compact poem rounded off by a mechanical repetition of the first stanza
to recall the initial synthesis. That poem would have been considerable. But
the stanza of the Lamb makes yet a further synthesis with that which has
gone before, and the poem as it stands has a unity that transcends the

original. Not only does Blake expand the vision once more to the infinity of night, but he /129/ extends the implications of the poem. And, after the stanza of the Lamb, the concluding stanza is no mere repetition; it gains new meaning from its context. The final stanza is controlled in its significance by the poetic experience that precedes it.

The first couplet of the interpolated stanza:

> When the stars threw down their spears,
> And water'd heaven with their tears,

seems to me to need little elucidation. The stars are a symbol of material power. In the throwing down of the spears the instruments of strife are cast aside, and pity assumed; and the Creator, no longer Los or Urizen, but the God of Innocence, smiles upon the triumph of the Lamb.

There is a loose development of this idea of the stars throwing down their spears in the poem *Morning* in the *Rossetti Ms.* 'Sweet Mercy' is leading the writer, and he urges his way,

> To find the Western path
> Right thro' the Gates of Wrath,

and when Mercy overcomes Wrath, and we come to 'the break of day',

> The war of swords & spears
> Melted by dewy tears
> Exhales on high;
>   (p. 137; 108.)

at dawn the spears of the stars melt in the sky. This link with the image of the dawn is interesting; for in *The Tyger* we have come through the 'forests of the night'.

In the symbol of the stars throwing down their spears, the symbolism of night implicit in *The Tyger* is itself used to express the triumph of Innocence over Experience, and the vision moves here, as it has already done in the earlier stanzas, from the spatial theme (the stars throwing down their spears) to the deed of creation, the handiwork—

> Did he smile his work to see?
> Did he who made the Lamb make thee?

The rejection of the war in infinity leads to the only two lines of complete Innocence, when the tyger and the Lamb exist in eternity together, in the whole of the *Songs of Experience*.

The stanza of the Lamb is closely related to the rest of the poem in its detail, as well as in its general implications. The line which /130/ precedes it directs the imagination to the clasping hand; and the throwing down of the spears is itself an action of a clasped hand. Moreover, the hand is an image paramount throughout the poem and another is the eye (cp. the fire of the tyger's eyes, and the immortal 'hand or eye'). This is relevant to the second line of stanza five, to the word tears. The third line maintains the relevance:

> Did he *smile* his work to *see*?

That line originally stood:

> And did he laugh his work to see.

And Blake was at pains to alter 'laugh' to 'smile', a change of major significance, that demonstrates the completeness of Blake's poetic control. The poem is silent except when the heart beats and the forge works; and laughter would have destroyed that quality of silence, and introduced a quite alien image—the mouth. As it stands, the smile is generated in the eyes, from the sight; and this, and the silence of the stanza, assimilate it into the rest of the poem (so much *does* depend on a single word in poetry) while its infinite serenity contrasts with the measured activity of the stanza before it.

The stanza of the Lamb is the only one in which not only the tyger of wrath and rebellion is brought to harmony, but the universe of stars and night as well. The tyger lies down with the Lamb. And from this the final stanza takes on an impulse and a direction not given to the opening of the poem, the meaning in the final stanza, and our reaction to it, are generated in, and dominated by, the poetic experience through which we have just come.

Martin K. Nurmi

Blake's Revisions of *The Tyger**

In Blake's Notebook drafts of *The Tyger* we have a valuable record of the growth of a great poem, a record which not only brings the poem itself into clearer focus but gives us as well another glimpse of the poet during a crucial but scantily documented period of his life. Yet, curiously enough, critics have largely neglected them. The fact that Blake revised this poem more than any other has been noticed, to be sure, and some critics have shown how a line or a stanza in the final poem is an improvement over earlier versions. But only one extended study of the drafts has been made, Joseph Wicksteed's attempt to reconstruct Blake's composition by association of ideas.[1] And that is incomplete: of the three full drafts of the poem (counting the final version as the third), and the additional drafts of two stanzas, Wicksteed studies thoroughly only the first draft and an additional draft of one stanza.

The present article is an attempt in some measure to fill in this critical gap, by tracing Blake's revisions through all his drafts, in order to clarify the poem's general meaning. In it I shall also offer a conjecture as to the occasion of the poem, based on the pattern in which it evolves, and shall include an accurate typographic transcription of Blake's MS. drafts of the poem.[2]

---

* Reprinted by permission of the Modern Language Association from *PMLA*, LXXI (1956), 669-685.

[1] *Blake's Innocence and Experience* (London, 1928), pp. 246-251. Stanley Gardner, in *Infinity on the Anvil* (Oxford, 1954), pp. 123-130, uses the drafts to some extent, to show the greater effectiveness of the final poem.

[2] Unfortunately, all published transcriptions of the drafts of this poem are either incomplete, simplified, or silently condensed, including that in Bunsho Jugaku's *A Bibliographical Study of William Blake's Note-Book* (Tokyo, 1953), which purports to correct previous transcriptions of the Notebook. A photographic facsimile of the Notebook has been published by Geoffrey Keynes, in *The Notebook of William Blake* (London, 1935), and a facsimile of the section of it containing *Songs of Experience* by Wicksteed, in *Blake's Innocence and Experience*. Blake's Notebook is frequently called the Rossetti MS., after D. G. Rossetti, who once owned it.

Because Wicksteed does not treat the drafts as a whole, he is led to view the evolution of *The Tyger* too simply, as an undeviating expansion of meaning and increase in poetic effectiveness. It would be more accurate to regard it as a kind of dialectical struggle in which Blake strives to bring his emblematic tiger's two "contraries"—its "deadly terrors" and the divinity in which it participates by having been created by an "immortal hand or eye"—into the "fearful symmetry" symbolized by the animal's natural symmetry of ferocity and beauty, and even by its con- /670/ trasting stripes.[3] This symmetry was the kernel of Blake's original conception, but he was not able to build his poem directly to embody it. If we follow his progress through his drafts, we will notice that his work falls into three stages in which this symmetry is significantly modulated. In the first stage he emphasizes the tiger's dreadfulness, portraying the beast as a cruel and bloody horror and asking pointed questions concerning its origin; in the second stage he swings to the opposite pole, shifting his emphasis to the tiger's divine origin by adding a stanza which rhetorically suggests that the tiger and the lamb do have a common creator and by omitting most of the tiger's dreadful attributes; in the third stage he retains the positive elements of the second stage, using the suggestion of the tiger's divine origin for the climax, but he also restores some of the dreadfulness of the first stage, though none of its horror, to effect a positively weighted synthesis of the two earlier stages in the complex affirmation of the final poem. Approached through its drafts, the final poem thus emerges quite clearly as a complex but essentially positive statement affirming the dread tiger's divinity, and not a probing of good and evil, as it has sometimes been interpreted.[4]

In the drafts Blake does probe the meaning of the tiger as a symbol of "evil"—in his ironic sense of the word—as a symbol of that creative cosmic energy so feared by the orthodox "angels" in all its manifestations. In the

---

[3] "Symmetry" could, of course, also be taken to refer more generally to the tiger's beautiful shape and harmonious design, but this meaning is not primary, since Blake is less interested in the tiger as a real animal than as a symbol of the coincidence of opposites.

[4] I do not advance this as a novel interpretation. Among the critics who interpret the poem as an affirmation are Wicksteed (p. 187); Gardner (pp. 129-130); Mark Schorer, in *William Blake: The Politics of Vision* (New York, 1946), pp. 250-251; Jacob Bronowski, in *William Blake: A Man Without a Mask* (London, 1944, 1954), pp. 116, 169; David V. Erdman, in *Blake: Prophet Against Empire* (Princeton, 1954), pp. 179-181. But the opinion that Blake is here probing good and evil is widely held. It is essentially the view expressed by S. Foster Damon, *William Blake, His Philosophy and Symbols* (London, 1924), pp. 276-278, and is shared by a series of notes in *Explicator* which attempt to explicate the imagery of the poem, especially that of the 5th stanza. See those by George W. Stone, Jr., Dec. 1942, no. 19; Ralph D. Eberly, Nov. 1949, no. 12; and Frederick A. Pottle, March 1950, no. 39. See also Kathleen Raine, "Who Made the Tyger?," *Encounter*, II (June 1954), 43-50.

drafts indeed, he seems to pass through some kind of spiritual crisis concerning it. For his difficulty in fixing the tiger's symmetry is not merely a compositional one. In one sense it is that, of course. But when the poet who had written the superbly controlled lyrics of *Poetical Sketches* and *Songs of Innocence* successively exaggerates the two aspects of his symbolic tiger's nature as much as Blake's earlier drafts show him to do, we may plausibly attribute his compositional difficulties to a difficulty in accepting the implications of the tiger's meaning for himself. In the first stage of composition, Blake's pointed questions concerning a cruel and horrible tiger are not the result of imprecise diction, for he ac- /671/ tually revised one stanza to make his questions more pointed; rather they hint that he was troubled and even repelled by his tiger's dreadfulness, despite his intention to show it as being harmonious with God's will. His transformation of this monster into the greatly ameliorated tiger of his second stage, who is only nominally dreadful, indeed almost benign, when compared with the tiger of either the first or third stage, similarly suggests that he overcame his initial doubts, experiencing such elation at being able to do so that he became even too optimistic. Finally, his adjustment of these two attitudes in the final poem seems to indicate that he had come to view the tiger's dreadfulness more philosophically than he was able to do in the first stage, and more realistically than he was able to do in the second.

That Blake went through some kind of crisis can be demonstrated from the drafts, but specifically what kind of crisis it was we can only conjecture. Several signs, however, seem to point to his revolutionary sympathies. From their position in the Notebook, the drafts of *The Tyger* appear to have been written sometime during 1792, or at the latest 1793,[5] the period of violence in France when many who had supported the revolution were having second thoughts about it. Since Blake seems to have conceived of tigers as natural symbols for energy, and even hinted at their connection with the revolutionary manifestation of energy, in *The Marriage of Heaven and Hell* (1790-93),[6] his bloody and repellent characterization

---

[5] They come near the end of those *Songs of Experience* which are written in the Notebook on the same page as the drafts of *London*, which may refer to the proclamation against seditious writings issued in May 1792 and again in Dec. (Erdman, p. 256), and they precede by 9 pp. the MS. poem usually called *Fayette*, which describes events in France through 25 Oct. 1792 (Erdman, pp. 167-168 n.). The accepted terminus ad quem for *Songs of Experience* (except for *To Tirzah*, added later) is 10 Oct. 1793, when they were advertised in Blake's *Prospectus*, though not all of the songs may have been included in that edition.

[6] See "Proverbs of Hell," no. 44: "The tygers of wrath are wiser than the horses of instruction." Also the fiery creature appearing "to the east, distant about three degrees" (the distance of Paris from London), which the angel's metaphysics distorts into Leviathan, has a tiger's forehead. (The beast who emerges from the sea in Rev. XIII. 2, the most plausible model for this one, was "like unto a leopard," but had the feet of a bear and the mouth of a lion.) *Blake's Poetry and Prose*, ed. Geoffrey Keynes (London,

of the tiger of the poem in the first stage of composition may show a temporary disillusionment with revolution, a disillusionment parallel to that expressed in the bitter quatrain sometimes added to the preludium of *America,* where the Bard shatters his harp in rage, "asham'd of his own song."[7] This possibility is supported by the indication that his mood changes to one of optimism when he /672/ writes, in his pivotal second stage, the crucial lines containing the symbolic action of stars throwing down their spears and weeping, for this action closely echoes his symbolic descriptions of the surrender and repentance of kings in both *The French Revolution* (1791) and *America* (1793).

This is not to imply that *The Tyger* is, after all, nothing more than a sublime piece of political allegory. Such an interpretation would both fail to square with our experience of the poem and mistake Blake's intention and method. *The Tyger* has many meanings, not only because it is an emblematic masterpiece which by itself supports a variety of valid interpretations, but because its context in Blake's thought as a whole gives it many. The poem describes an apocalypse—by definition a vast and inclusive event—which occurs in a cosmos knit by interpenetrating "correspondences" uniting any one event with all others. No single interpretation, therefore, whether political, religious, ethical, or sexual, can be sufficient in itself. On the other hand, these considerations do not prevent us from talking about the poem concretely. Its very inclusiveness of meaning enables us to approach it through any relevant particular meanings, and to suggest that it may have been connected with a specific point in history, without implying any limitation of the poem as a whole.

I mentioned that Blake's introduction of stars and heavens into the poem marks a turning point in his composition. Since we shall have to be quite clear about this symbolism as we consider the drafts in detail, and since it has puzzled many readers, some explication of it here will be useful. The lines in question are those later forming the fifth stanza:

> When the stars threw down their spears,
> And water'd heaven with their tears,
> Did he smile his work to see?
> Did he who made the Lamb make thee? (p. 73)

We can approach these symbols most clearly and concretely through Blake's use of them in his contemporary historical prophecies. In his work in general, stars and heavens symbolize the rigidly categorical restrictions

1948), pp. 184, 189-190. Unless otherwise indicated, page references to Blake's works will cite this edition.

[7] See Erdman, pp. 264, 267-268 n. This same uncertainty is reflected later in Los's ambivalence toward Orc in *The Book of Urizen* (pp. 230-231) and *The Four Zoas* (pp. 295-296).

imposed upon man by laws derived from abstract reason, and the weeping of stars symbolizes at the cosmic level an apocalyptic melting or breaking down of these barriers separating man from his own humanity, a return of man from the "forests of night."8 But in the works /673/ of 1791-93 an important particular meaning of these symbols, as Erdman has shown, is that of political repression, specifically the agents of repression, kings and nobles.9 In *The French Revolution*, the king's bosom expands "like starry heaven" (p. 169) when he assembles the nobles, the "Heavens of France" (p. 175); aristocratic privilege is a "marble built heaven"; its destruction a "starry harvest"; and the king's armies, who are to defend the heavens, are "starry hosts" (p. 170). In *America* the thrones of kings are similarly "heav'nly thrones," and Urizen, the god of kings, sits "above all heavens" (pp. 207-208).

In these same works are to be found several echoes of the action in the fifth stanza of *The Tyger*. Blake, when he describes the repentance or defeat of tyrants, consistently shows the starry forces throwing down their spears (and swords and muskets) and weeping. In *The French Revolution* the Abbé de Sieyès, as the voice of the people, hopes that the king's soldier will "Throw down . . . [his] sword and musket, / And run and embrace the meek peasant," and predicts that when this happens, the "Nobles shall hear and shall weep, and put off / . . . the crown of oppression" (p. 176). A similar throwing down of weapons and weeping occurs twice in *America*, not as a hope but as an accomplished fact, and it is, furthermore, produced by the appearance of the fiery Orc, just as the action in our poem is brought about through the creation of the burning tiger. When the spirit of Orc inspires the Americans, "The British soldiers thro' the thirteen states sent up a howl / Of anguish, threw their swords & muskets to the earth, & ran" (p. 206). And a little later, when the red fires of Orc have driven the plagues sent upon the Americans back upon George III himself, the royal forces "sent up a howl of anguish and threw off their hammer'd mail, / And cast their swords & spears to earth" (p. 207). When this happens, Urizen adds to their tears of anguish by weeping himself; indeed, he literally waters the heavens above which he sits, shedding tears in a grotesque "deluge piteous" (pp. 207-208).

No one would argue that this symbolic action in the historical prophecies is exactly equivalent in meaning—or effect—to the action in the

---

8 *Europe*, p. 216. Famous exceptions to stars as symbols of repression are illustration XIV to Job, "When the morning Stars sang together, and all the Sons of God shouted for joy," where Blake is, of course, illustrating another's work, and the early lyric "To the Morning Star" in *Poetical Sketches* (1783). On the place of stars in Blake's symbolic cosmography see Damon, pp. 143-144. 9

9 Erdman, pp. 15, 153, 178-180, 436-437.

fifth stanza of *The Tyger*. But the pattern of the starry kings' armies throwing down their weapons and weeping, whether in repentance or in the unrepentant anguish of defeat, is similar enough to the action in the first two lines of the stanza to indicate that these lines do at one level describe a victory for political liberty, if only as a symptom or a result of the apocalypse.[10] And the context of the rest of the poem shows that this /674/ victory is a result of the creation of the dread tiger. Knowing Blake's republican sympathy and the transcendent values he attached to political liberty, we can be certain at this level that the creator of a tiger which could thus advance the cause of freedom was none other than "he who made the Lamb," and we can be just as certain that this creator smiled "his work to see." Moreover, because the unity of Blake's cosmos assures us of consistency in the general import of his symbolism through all of its levels of meaning, we can be confident that the fifth stanza shows the dread tiger to be not only a divine creation but also, despite its dreadfulness, an aspect of the divine will, at whatever level we read the poem.[11]

With this much preparation, let us then turn to examine the three stages of Blake's composition in some detail. The first two stages are to be found in the Notebook, and the third in the final poem itself.

I

The first stage consists of the first draft (p. 109, col. 2 of the Notebook) and the revisions of the second stanza of this draft, the

---

[10] That this stanza includes an historical meaning has been suggested by Schorer (pp. 250-251) and Erdman (pp. 178-180).

[11] As has often been noted, the action of the stars throwing down their spears, both in *The Tyger* and in v. 224 (p. 299) of *The Four Zoas*—where Urizen recounts his defeat—is related to Milton's account of the war in Heaven. The relation, however, is a complicated one, and in a way inverted. The tiger is not to be equated with Satan-Urizen; he is, if anything, closer to Orc. And the action in *The Four Zoas*, as the historical allegory in night V makes clear, has also an apocalyptic aspect, in Blake's sense of that term (p. 647), for Urizen is recapitulating the collapse of the hosts of reaction in the American war and after, giving an account that matches the last page of *America* and the first of *Europe* (Erdman, pp. 343-349). If we wish a Miltonic-Scriptural equivalent for the tiger, it must be the militant Christ—as the Lamb is the forgiving Christ. Prof. Erdman has called my attention to the fact that the plot of *Europe* hinges on the distinction between these two aspects of Christ. That the tiger is an active force fighting for "divine humanity" is further shown by Blake's re-use of the action of the 5th stanza, with the actors and mood changed, in night IX of *The Four Zoas*, where he spells out, as it were, the apocalyptic implications of *The Tyger*. This time it is the "tygers from the forests" (as well as horses, bulls, and lions) who put aside their weapons. Not, however, in defeat and sorrow, or even in Urizen's mixed mood of repentance, but in the unalloyed joy of victors in the final apocalypse: They "throw *away* [not down, italics mine]/The spear, the bow, the gun, the mortar"; and, instead of weeping, they "sing" and "sieze the instruments of harmony" (p. 355).

Notebook) and the revisions of the second stanza of this draft, the
interlineal revisions as well as the new draft of the stanza on the page
opposite (Notebook, p. 108, col. 1; the pages run backwards because Blake
was using his Notebook in reverse at this time).[12]

That Blake's initial attitude toward the dreadfulness of the tiger and his
creator is a troubled one is shown by his repellent portrayal of the tiger in
the deleted stanza of the first draft (the fourth stanza in order /675/ of
composition, but heavily deleted, and omitted as the stanzas were later
numbered). "And when thy heart began to beat / What dread hand & what
dread feet," he asks,

> Could fetch it from the furnace deep
> And in thy horrid ribs dare steep
> In the well of sanguine woe
> In what clay & in what mould
> Were thy eyes of fury rolld

Even though Blake is evidently thinking on paper here, trying lines as they
come, we can scarcely take expressions such as "horrid ribs," "sanguine
woe," and "eyes of fury" to be merely crudely exaggerated
characterizations of a dread power that was viewed as a means to Eden.
Blake had too much control to be guilty of this much exaggeration even in
a rough draft. Nor does this kind of horror form a part of his conception
of revolutionary energy. Though Orc in *America* is "terrible," he never
becomes "horrid," and though his raging fires produce tears of anguish
among the enemies of liberty, they never produce anything remotely
approaching "sanguine woe." The tiger's dreadfulness is appalling here, we
must conclude, because Blake was unable to accept it easily; an implied
rejection of it crept into his verse even as he wrote to justify it as being
symmetrical with God's purpose.

This attitude of uncertainty is maintained and given more explicit
expression by the revision of the second stanza of this draft. In the stanza
as originally written, dreadfulness is general and evocative:

> In what distant deeps or skies
> Burnt the fire of thine eyes
> On what wings dare he aspire
> What the hand dare sieze the fire

It was consistent with Blake's intention in the poem as a whole that
dreadfulness should not be too horrible and that the questions asked about
the tiger should be rhetorically general enough, as they are here, not to

---

[12] All page references to the Notebook cite the MS. pages.

demand answers other than those supplied by the image of the tiger itself. Indeed, Blake used this original evocative form of the stanza in the final poem, where he realizes his intention.

But he does not, in the first stage of the composition, allow this form of the stanza to stand. Evidently the rather generalized questions in these lines, however appropriate to his purpose in the poem, are not sharp enough to express his real attitude toward the tiger's dreadful aspect. For he makes interlineal revisions which change the question in the first two lines from one which asks evocatively *where* the tiger got the fire of /676/ his eyes to one which asks more pointedly *whether* he got it from "distant deeps or skies"; futhermore, the fire now becomes cruel:

> Burnt in distant deeps or skies
> The cruel fire of thine eyes

Did the "cruel" fire come from the Devil (deeps) or from God (skies)? Or did it have an eternal source at all? These questions demand an answer; the original question does not. The original question, to be sure, asks us formally to name the source of the fire, but it does not ask whether the fire has an eternal source, for it assumes that it has. It asks only from which of a number of distant deeps or skies it came, calling attention to the transcendent qualities of the tiger's eyes. A real answer is demanded by the revised question, whichever way it is read. Read one way it asks us to choose between deeps and skies as alternatives and may even urge deeps, since it tells us that the fire is cruel. Read the other way it flatly demands an answer of "yes" or "no."

This sharp question was the one Blake wanted to ask in this stage, for though he struck out the revisions made between the lines, he transcribed this stanza as revised, on the following page (Notebook, p. 108, col. 1). The position of the transcribed stanza on the page indicates that it belongs with the first draft.[13]

II

Blake's second stage of composition is represented by a new stanza (Notebook, p. 108, col. 1), written below and presumably after the

---

[13] Transcribing this stanza, the uppermost entry on the left-hand column of p. 108, would very likely have been Blake's next work on the poem after writing the first draft. This is Wicksteed's opinion (p. 248). Keynes, however, in his printed versions of the Notebook, both in *Notebook*, pp. 17-19, and in *The Writings of William Blake* (London, 1925), I, 231-233, places this stanza in the 2nd full draft of the poem, as does Jugaku (p. 81). There is no indication that it belongs there.

transcription of the revised second stanza, and by the second full draft of
the poem (p. 108, col. 2). In this stage Blake swings to the other pole,
displaying such enthusiasm over the tiger's positive side that he pushes its
dreadfulness into the background.

The crucial lines of this stage are those of the new stanza (eventually to
become the fifth stanza of the final poem), in which Blake shifts away
from the tiger to introduce the results of its creation, in the symbolism of
stars and heavens. (The number 5 evidently indicates the place of the
stanza in the final draft; the deleted 3 was originally a stanza number and
then left as a line number. Words crossed out by the poet are here
italicized.) /677/

> 5   dare he *smile laugh*
> 3   And *did he laugh* his work to see
>   *ankle*
>   *What the shoulder what the knee*
> Dare
> 4 *Did* he who made the lamb make thee
> 1   When the stars threw down their spears
> 2   And waterd heaven with their tears

These lines show a marked change in mood. Blake apparently conceives the
whole poem somewhat differently than before, since he proposes to
substitute for his original third stanza, which had described the sinews of a
dread tiger's heart, a stanza which he begins (taking the lines in order of
composition) in such a positive and joyful mood that he cannot decide
whether to ask if the creator laughed or only smiled. He is simply not in
the mood for dread, and when he attempts to carry on more or less in his
original vein in the second line, he is led away from the creator's forging
and twisting shoulder to the bathos of knee and even ankle. In the third
line ("Did [or Dare] he," etc.) he gets to the heart of the matter in the
central question of the poem. But the answer is pretty clear in his mind,
for, in context with the mood implied by his indecision over "smile" and
"laugh" and the bathetic "ankle," this question scarcely could be answered
"no." The answer is, in any case, made clearer in the following two lines
by the apocalyptic symbolism of the stars throwing down their spears and
weeping.[14]

Blake's rearrangement of the lines by numbering them 3, 4, 1, and 2, and

[14] Blake probably intended the lines about stars and spears to begin the stanza and
supply a context for the other questions even before he wrote them. Coming after the
3rd line, they would not only be badly anticlimactic but would make the stanza shift
from the central question implicit in the whole poem, to make the stanza ask whether
the creation of the tiger was simultaneous with the stars' throwing down their spears.

his omission of the bathetic line, make the stanza firmer and much more clearly positive in mood. Placing the lines about stars and heavens first qualifies the question concerning the creator's response to his dread creation in such a way that the answer is obvious: "Did he smile (or laugh) his work to see[?]" no longer asks simply whether the creator was in general pleased with his tiger, but asks more specifically whether he was pleased with it *when* it caused the stars to throw down their spears and weep. Put this way, the question becomes obviously rhetorical. And the line ending the stanza in the new arrangement, "Did (or Dare) he who made the lamb make thee[?]" becomes a positive rhetorical climax which sums up the whole poem.[15] /678/

This mood of certainty is maintained in the second full draft of the poem (Notebook, p. 108, col. 2). In this draft, a fair copy written out without revisions and spaced on the page as if it were final, Blake omits most of the dreadfulness of the first stage. He omits altogether the second stanza; he omits the bloody deleted stanza, and thereby also reduces the questions of the third stanza, "What dread hand & what dread feet[?]" to mere suggestions of dreadfulness, for he has removed the verb needed to complete these questions; and he omits the next to the last stanza, which had asked what "dread grasp" could clasp the "deadly terrors" of the tiger's brain. The result of these omissions is a poem of only four stanzas, in which all the dreadfulness is in the ambiguous suggestions of the strophic first and last stanzas—powerful suggestions in the final poem in context with the restored stanzas, but ambiguous by themselves—and in the truncated question without a verb. We must now accept the tiger's fearful aspect merely because we are told that there is a fearful symmetry in him and that his creator has a dread hand and a dread foot. Blake seems to rush over the tiger's unpleasant aspect to get to the rhetorical affirmation in the new stanza, which is included here. In this abbreviated poem the new stanza overbalances the tiger's symmetry so much that it no longer seems very fearful. It is not because of Blake's usually casual orthography that "Immortal" is capitalized in the first stanza of this draft; he wishes to stress the tiger's divine aspect.

III

In his third stage, in the final poem itself, Blake retains the assurance he had gained in the second, using the stanza about stars and spears as the climax of the poem. But now he is more realistic about the tiger, for he

---

[15] For what it may be worth as an indication of the importance Blake attached to the ideas introduced in this stanza, this is the only stanza of the drafts which he did not cross out with the vertical lines he used to mark engraved stanzas.

restores some of its original dreadfulness. He restores the stanzas beginning
"In what distant deeps or skies" and "What the hammer? what the chain?"
(the second and fourth stanza of the final poem), to give the tiger's creator
once more a "dread grasp" and the tiger itself a brain of "deadly terrors."
But if he is more realistic than in the second stage, he is also more
philosophical than in the first. He no longer portrays the tiger's
dreadfulness with the harsh immediacy of his original characterization, but
brings it into perspective by ameliorating and generalizing it. He does not
restore the bloody stanza of the first draft, and consequently allows the
truncated questions, "And what dread hand? and what dread feet?" (stanza
three) to remain mere suggestions of dreadfulness, grammatically
incomplete, as they had been in the second draft.[16] And though /679/ he
does restore the second stanza of the first draft, he uses it in its evocative
form, in which it asks vaguely *where* the tiger got the fire of his eyes, no
longer cruel. Viewed against its drafts, the final poem shows Blake to have
a tight control of his materials because he can perceive clearly and steadily
the unity underlying the tiger's symmetry: The tiger *is* dreadful, but its
dreadfulness is an "accident" and not its "substance," to use one of his
favorite philosophical distinctions; its substance is power, the power of that
energy which will return man to Eden.

This conceptual unity is embodied not only in the final image but in the
very structure of the poem itself. The structure of the final poem almost
perfectly illustrates Blake's hard dictum that a truly unified work of art
must have its unity "as much in the Part as in the Whole" (p. 582), and
reminds one of the structure of a Gothic cathedral (to Blake "living form "
p. 583), in which each stone, often even each slate in the roof, may be said

---

[16] These questions are grammatically complete in the versions of the poem given by
Benjamin Malkin in *A Father's Memoirs of His Child* and Allan Cunningham in *Lives of
the Most Eminent British Painters*, Vol. II. Malkin gives the line as "What dread hand
forged thy dread feet?" (in Arthur Symons, *William Blake*, New York, 1907, p. 326),
and Cunningham, as "What dread hand formed thy dread feet?" (Symons, p. 394). With
this and one other less important exception, Malkin's version agrees with extant printed
versions, and his alteration of the line may have been approved by Blake, whom he knew
personally; Mona Wilson seems certain that Blake did approve it (*The Life of William
Blake*, London, 1948, p. 192). But Cunningham's text of the poem as a whole departs so
far from any other version ("spears" become "spheres," for instance, and the last stanza
is omitted altogether) as to indicate that it is simply inaccurate, perhaps written from
memory. His version of the lines in question, however, does happen to agree with the
only alteration which we know Blake to have authorized, found in one extant issue of
Innocence and Experience (copy *P* in Geoffrey Keynes and Edwin Wolf II, *William
Blake's Illuminated Books*, New York, 1954, p. 61), in which the last line of the stanza is
changed in ink to read, "What dread hand Formd thy dread feet?" All of these
alterations belong to a later period. Malkin's *Memoirs* was published in 1806,
Cunningham's *Lives* in 1830, and copy *P* of *Innocence and Experience* is dated by
Keynes and Wolf as 1802 or later (p. 52).

to support its own weight. For each of the questions of which the poem is composed, even those which show the tiger's dreadfulness, provides its own answer, not as simple rhetorical questions would, but by contributing to the complex but unified total image in which all questions are answered. The tiger thus comes to be its own justification.

From the vantage point of the final poem it is easy to see why Blake's overbalanced moods in his first two stages prevented him from achieving a symmetrical tiger, for the final poem shows that both aspects of the symmetry must be advanced at the same time. The second stanza cannot be omitted, as it had been in the exultant second stage, nor can it ask the sharply limiting questions it had asked in the first. It must be there in its evocative form, not only to support the suggestion of immortality given in the first stanza, but to supply a spacious context for /680/ the dreadfulness in the following two stanzas, so that the image they build up can become awesome, and not merely dreadful. In this context the third stanza (used in the second stage almost as a hasty concession that the tiger had an unpleasant aspect) and the fourth stanza (omitted in the second stage) bring out the tiger's dreadfulness, by showing its "deadly terrors" to be the work of a dread hand twisting and forging; but at the same time, paradoxically, they make the tiger seem actually less dreadful, because it becomes more and more awesome, as they build the total image. As a result, the rhetorical affirmation of the fifth stanza no longer shifts the reader arbitrarily to the tiger's positive side, as it had done in the second stage, but culminates the characterization of the preceding stanzas, forming a kind of climactic modulation to a major key which clearly and triumphantly provides a final resolution to the progression that had been moving toward resolution all along. The real climax, of course, which resolves everything, is the word "Dare" that is substituted for "Could" in the closing return to the strophic stanza. Coming after the image of the tiger is completed, the last two lines are not a question, not even a rhetorical one, but a cry of wonder.

Thus the final poem is essentially positive. The dread it expresses, though real—and deplorable, apart from its role in melting starry repression—has been assimilated to the larger imaginative vision of the poet-prophet, "Who Present, Past, & Future, sees" (p. 65). As one of the *Songs of Innocence and of Experience, The Tyger* belongs to that complex stratum of lyrics composed of poems like *The Little Black Boy* and *The Chimney Sweeper* (of *Innocence*), which shows both states at once. And it expresses the general idea that the ultimate Edenic Innocence is to be attained only through the bitterness of Experience. But it also goes beyond this conception of the "two contrary states of the human soul," to show that Innocence, when it is in danger of being destroyed by the repression of a fallen "God & his Priest & King" (p. 70), may even temporarily take

on some of the characteristics of its contrary state, becoming transformed
into a wrathful energy which may itself occasion bitterness. The lamb, as
Schorer observes, turns "into something else, indeed into the tiger" (p.
250). To attain the dawn, man may have to act in "the forests of the
night." In its immediate context in Blake's lyrics of this period, *The Tyger*
thus shows the apotheosis of that armed Innocence portrayed in a MS.
lyric that comes three pages later in the Notebook (p. 105), where the sun,
a symbol of peaceful Innocence throughout the songs,[17] becomes wrathful,
"Clothd in robes of blood & gold... Crownd with warlike fires & raging
desires." But this wrathful state is a temporary one. As Blake expresses it
some years later in /681/ another poem (Notebook, p. 12), transforming
the symbolism of the fifth stanza of *The Tyger*, the path leads through the
"Gates of Wrath" to the "break of day," where the corporeal war of
"swords & spears / Melted by dewy tears / Exhales on high..."

It seems to me that the change of mood which we have observed Blake
to pass through in his first two stages can be most easily accounted for as
reflecting his responses to events in France in the late summer and early
autumn of 1792. Several lines of evidence converge to suggest this: the
date of the drafts, the historical echoes in the pivotal fifth stanza, and
above all the fact that the course of the revolution in this period was such
that it could—and did—arouse this kind of response among humanitarian
republicans.

Such cruel excesses of revolutionary energy as the Rising of the 10th of
August and the September Massacres furnish a plausible occasion for
Blake's troubled mood in the first stage. There was always something of
the "gentle visionary" about Blake, and he must have deplored these early
terrors, despite his ardent Jacobinism. Though his apocalypses may
sometimes stream with blood (e.g., the end of *Milton*), he preferred to
think of revolutions as bloodless, hoping in *The French Revolution* that the
struggle would end by the king's soldier simply embracing the "meek
peasant." Even in *America*, where he must treat a military victory won by
American armies, he would rather not show the Americans as actually
fighting; they merely "rush together," owing their victory to the fact of
their solidarity and to the spiritual manifestation of revolution in the
flaming Orc.

Then in late September came news that violence was apparently over,
news which could have prompted the shift in mood seen in Blake's second
stage. Viewed prophetically, such events as the defeat of the Austrians at
Valmy on the 20th (to which Erdman, p. 178, has called attention in
connection with the fifth stanza), the formation of the National

---

17 See especially "The Little Black Boy," "The Chimney Sweeper" (of *Innocence*),
"Introduction" to *Experience*, "Earth's Answer," and "The Voice of the Ancient Bard."

Convention on the 21st and the announcement of the French Republic on the 22nd must have made the attainment of Innocence seem close enough to cast the bloody actions of August and mid-September pretty well into the background. This view, according to Wordsworth and Coleridge, was even typical. The "lamentable crimes" of the September Massacres, writes Wordsworth, remembering the period after the announcement of the Republic,

> were past
> Earth free from them for ever, as was thought,—
> Ephemeral monsters, to be seen but once!
> Things that could only show themselves and die.18/682/

"The dissonance ceased," recalls Coleridge, "and all seemed calm and bright..."19

Blake is not, to be sure, writing merely a revolutionary lyric. His tiger is not another Orc, another portrayal of the spirit of revolt, but something much more inclusive, a symbol showing the creative power of energy, even of wrathful energy, wherever it appears. But because the revolution was for Blake a crucial contemporary manifestation of energy, events in the progress of the revolution would affect even his larger conception.20

For Blake to have been thus affected by contemporary events, his Notebook would have had to lie idle for a period of ten days or even several weeks, since the MS. drafts are on successive pages. This is easily possible. He did not write in his Notebook exclusively or constantly, but used it at this time for lyrics, which, according to H. M. Margoliouth, were written in response to events of one kind or another.21 Moreover, if his uncertainty concerning such an important concept as that of energy was unresolved during his first stage, it is unlikely that he could work very productively until it was resolved, in the second stage. That an interruption did occur is suggested, indeed, by the appearance of the pages of the

18 *Prelude* (1850), ed. Ernest de Selincourt (London, 1926), x.41-47.

19 "France: An Ode," *Poems*, ed. Ernest Hartley Coleridge (London, 1912), p. 245.

20 The Orc component of the tiger may be seen in the general similarities between the tiger and Orc in *America*, who, like the tiger, burns in the night as if he had been forged, glowing "as the wedge / Of iron heated in the furnace" (p. 202), and whose origin is a little ambiguously either in the Satanic deeps or the divine Atlantic mountains (p. 202). Very bloody revolutionary tigers indeed are associated with Orc in *Europe*, where Enitharmon's premature belief that Eden had come—a situation parallel to Blake's 2nd stage of composition—is shattered by the resumption of strife (p. 219). These tigers, however, are far removed from the tiger of the poem, representing a limit of this use of the symbol by Blake. Blake's later disillusionment with Orc in 1801 (as Napoleon—Erdman, p. 292) is parallel to his use of the "forms of tygers & of Lions" to show men "dishumaniz'd" by war in night VI of *The Four Zoas* (p. 303).

21 *William Blake* (London, 1951), p. 54. Margoliouth remarks that the occasion of *The Tyger* is unknown, but believes that this poem too is occasional (p. 58).

MS.—and even the appearance of a MS. page could conceivably have had some significance for the inventor of "illuminated printing." Whereas the first draft ends a page crowded with lyrics, the other drafts occupy a page that is otherwise blank, except for a light sketch. The empty space at the top of the. second page, coming after the profusion of poems on the first, thus seems a visual parallel to the mournful and unproductive "blank in Nature" declared by Los in *Milton* (p. 383).

Blake's last revision is another matter. The final poem cannot be accounted for as a response to specific events. Though the Terror of late 1792 and early 1793 could have shown him that his relatively mild /683/ tiger of the second stage was premature, his restoration of dreadfulness to the poem in its final version does not show the influence of events—and certainly not of events like the Terror—as do his exaggerations of the two earlier stages. On the contrary, Blake's being able to handle dreadfulness and assimilate it in the unified symmetry of the final poem shows him to gain precisely that control of his material which his concern with revolution seems to have prevented him from gaining in his earlier stages. He is now able to transcend the limitations of specific events and give his symbol the comprehensive scope of an "eternal principle." This is the result of hard thought, not of events. Blake can now give the tiger's dreadfulness symbolic distance because he can see it in a perspective in which it no longer has the immediacy of an issue. And he can portray its symmetry as containing a really fearful component because he can see clearly and fully, at this point, the place of the tiger in the divine plan.

Transcription of the Drafts of Blake's "The Tyger"

First draft, Rossetti MS., p. 109 (*italics indicate deletions*)

The Tyger

1 Tyger Tyger burning bright
    In the forests of the night
    What immortal hand or eye
Dare   *Could* frame thy fearful symmetry

    Burnt in
2 In what[1] distant deeps or skies
The cruel *Burnt the* fire of thine eyes
    On what wings dare he aspire
    What the hand dare sieze the fire

---

[1] "In what" deleted, but deletion line erased.

3 And what shoulder & what art
   Could twist the sinews of thy heart
   And when thy heart began to beat
   What dread hand & what dread feet

   Could fetch it from the furnace deep
   And in thy horrid ribs dare steep
   In the well of sanguine woe
   In what clay & in what mould
   Were thy eyes of fury rolld   /684/

   Where   where
4 *What* the hammer *what* the chain
   In what furnace was thy brain
                                              dread grasp
   What the anvil what *the arm arm grasp clasp*
Dare   *Could* its deadly terrors *clasp grasp* clasp

6 Tyger Tyger burning bright
   In the forests of the night
   What immortal hand & eye
          frame
   Dare *form* thy fearful symmetry

[The MS has a vertical deletion line reaching from the first line of the first stanza through the first line of the sixth.]

   Additional stanzas on opposite page (p. 108), column 1 of the note book

   Burnt in distant deeps or skies
   The cruel fire of thine eyes
   Could heart descend or wings aspire
   What the hand dare sieze the fire
      [Three vertical deletion lines.]

5 dare he *smile laugh*
3 And *did*[2] *he laugh* his work to see
                  ankle
   What the shoulder what the knee
Dare
4 *Did* he who made the lamb make thee

---

2 Above "did" is an illegible blotch, perhaps a deletion.

1 When the stars threw down their spears
2 And waterd heaven with their tears

Second full draft on page 108, column 2

Tyger Tyger burning bright
In the forests of the night
What Immortal hand & eye
Dare frame thy fearful symmetry

And what shoulder & what art
Could twist the sinews of thy heart
And when thy heart began to beat
What dread hand & what dread feet

When the stars threw down their spears
And waterd heaven with their tears
Did he smile his work to see
Did he who made the lamb make thee   /685/

Tyger Tyger burning bright
In the forests of the night
What immortal hand & eye
Dare frame thy fearful symmetry

[Three vertical deletion lines, one crossing the other two.]

The Final Form of Blake's "The Tyger"

Tyger! Tyger! burning bright
In the forests of the night,
What immortal hand or eye
Could frame thy fearful symmetry?

In what distant deeps or skies
Burnt the fire of thine eyes?
On what wings dare he aspire?
What the hand dare sieze the fire?

And what shoulder, & what art,
Could twist the sinews of thy heart?

And when thy heart began to beat,
What dread hand? & what dread feet?

What the hammer? what the chain?
In what furnace was thy brain?
What the anvil? what dread grasp
Dare its deadly terrors clasp?

When the stars threw down their spears,
And water'd heaven with their tears,
Did he smile his work to see?
Did he who made the Lamb make thee?

Tyger! Tyger! burning bright
In the forests of the night
What immortal hand or eye,
Dare frame thy fearful symmetry?

Hazard Adams

"The Tyger" as an Example*

"The Tyger" is a poem of rather simple form, clearly and cleanly proportioned, all of its statements contributing to a single, sustained, dramatic gesture. Read aloud, it is powerful enough to move many listeners (small children, for example) without their having much understanding of the poem beyond its expression of a dramatic situation. But Blake warns us that there is a great gulf between simplicity and insipidity. The total force of the poem comes not only from its immediate rhetorical power but also from its symbolical structure.

Blake's image of the tiger, at first sensuous, is to continued inspection symbolic. Things which burn brightly, even tigers, can be thought of as either purifying something or being purified. In the dark of night, in a forest, a tiger's eyes would seem to burn. The tiger's coat suggests this same conflagration. In any case, Blake is trying to establish a brilliance about his image which he elsewhere associates, not surprisingly, with the apocalyptic figure of his minor prophecies, Orc:

> But terrible Orc, when he beheld the morning in the east,
> Shot from the heights of Enitharmon,
> And in the vineyards of red France appear'd the light of his fury.
> [K244-45]†

There are many examples of the same imagery throughout the prophecies. Another visual image which Blake may be suggesting here is consistent with

---

* Reprinted from *William Blake: A Reading of the Shorter Poems* (Seattle: University of Washington Press, 1963), pp. 58-74, by permission of the publisher. Copyright 1963, University of Washington Press.

† *The Complete Writings of William Blake*, ed. Geoffrey Keynes (London, 1957), hereafter referred to as K.

what /59/ we shall see in the nature of the tiger itself. In many religious paintings (and in Blake's own work, the popularly mistitled "Glad Day," for example)[1] the central figure seems to be emerging from or surrounded by a vast light: figuratively he "burns." Visually the fire image suggests immediate violence; traditionally it suggests some sort of purgatorial revelation.

The forests of the poem represent those famous mythological areas inhabited by blatant beasts, lost knights, and various spiritual wanderers and travelers. These forests *belong to* the night: Blake clearly invites us to read his line symbolically. For Blake, night suggests the delusion of material substance and the absence of the kind of light that surrounds revelation. There is a violent contrast between light and darkness, between the tiger and its surroundings, and the reader recognizes that the forest and the night are to be thought of ib a derogatory way. The tiger, on the other hand, is presented ambiguously. In spite of its natural viciousness, it also suggests clarity and energy. If the reader has had prolonged experience with poetry and mythology, other associations will sharpen these ideas. He will perhaps associate the "forests of the night" with the traditional dark night or dark journey of the soul through the dens of demons and beasts. The tiger's brightness may suggest the force which the sun so often symbolizes in mythology. If the reader has read Dante, he may associate the forests with Dante's descent from the dark wood into the underworld; if he has read Goethe, he may notice a striking symbolic relationship between Blake's imagery and the imagery of enclosure in *Faust*—the forest, the study, the cave, the circle. Finally, if he has read Blake's own work, he will know that since the fall of man was a fall into a material world, he may associate the night with matter. In forests in the darkness men are trapped in an enclosure similar to Plato's cave, hobbled by the growing rubbish of materialism, blocked off from light by material substance. Men stand in forests surrounded by webs of leaves, limbs, vines, and bracken (Blake's illustrations provide ample evidence for such a symbolic interpretation of fallen life). Blake's prophecies work toward a similar expression of this idea in expanded form. In *The Book of Urizen*, Urizen, the arch-materialist of Blake's myth, traps himself in webbed enclosures similar to jungles. In *The Four Zoas* he sits in his "web of deceitful religion." /60/ The forest is also a symbol of the natural cycle of growth and decay in the fallen, natural world. It therefore represents not only spatial but also temporal enclosure. In his later prophecies Blake refers to the fallen world in its material, spatial form as the "mundane shell." Its opacity prevents man from seeing

---

[1] See David V. Erdman, *Blake: Prophet Against Empire* (Princeton, N.J.: Princeton University Press, 1954), p. 6, for an explanation of how it came to be so titled.

through to eternity. The time-form of the fallen world Blake calls the "circle of destiny," the world falsely seen in the spirit of materialistic determinism. The stars, which enter our poem in stanza 5, are a part of the concave surface of the mundane shell where man is trapped, and their movements represent the delusory, mechanical aspects of time. This shell is also a kind of egg, holding an embryo capable eventually of breaking the shell and leaping into real life free of the cycles of time and the enclosures of space.

In *The Four Zoas*, night symbolizes the history of the fallen world—its time-form, the circle of destiny. The archetypal man of Blake's prophetic books, Albion, a primordial giant symbolizing the human world, succumbs to sleep at the time of the fall and awakens only at the last judgment. In an early scheme for *The Four Zoas* Blake divided the history of the fallen world into nine "nights," each a historical cycle; and he subtitled his poem "The Death and Judgment of the Ancient Man, A Dream in Nine Nights." The fallen world is therefore a nightmare in the mind of Albion, who is afflicted by materialist delusions: for the materialist, the tiger appears out of darkness, a nightmarish figure, bright and violent, perhaps the vehicle of that terrible judgment he has been taught to believe in. What the tiger is to the visionary the poem is about to tell us, but in a subtler way.

Now all of the symbolic relationships that I have suggested may not be apparent in a cursory reading *in vacuo*. As the reader acquaints himself with the poem's clearly symbolic diction, the symbolical and allegorical tradition in western poetry, and finally Blake's own symbolical world, the poem gathers force. It is true that the reader is, to a certain degree, reading back and away from the poem into the world from which it has come, but even this is consistent with Blake's own view of the world: Man creates the world by the process of imagination; reading back and away from the poem is also reading back and *into* one's own mind. In one sense, at least, Blake wrote poems that the reader himself creates.

A reading of Blake's early drafts of "The Tyger" in the Rossetti MS reveals a rather important metamorphosis of the attitude of the speaker of the poem. /61/ Certain phrases from these drafts, later deleted, suggest that the speaker's attitude as Blake first conceived it was more clearly one of failure to understand and consequent fear of the tiger.[2] For example:

---

2 My point is corroborated, I think, by Martin Nurmi ("Blake's Revisions of *The Tyger*," *PMLA*, LXXI, No. 4 [September, 1956], 669-85), though he puts it with a different emphasis: "Blake [can portray] the tiger's symmetry as containing a really fearful component because he can see clearly and fully at this point the place of the tiger in the divine plan." From my point of view it would be better to say that Blake can portray the tiger's symmetry as having visionary beauty for this reason.

> What dread hand and what dread feet?
> Could fetch it from the furnace deep
> And in thy horrid ribs dare steep
> In the well of sanguine woe.

The hellish imagery of these lines (Blake contended, after all, that hell was a mental state), the reference to horrid ribs (one might compare the references to the ribs of Urizen in *The Book of Urizen*), and deadly terrors strongly suggest that the tiger is a product of a *real* hell and a *real* deathliness. Subsequently several of these images were eliminated from the poem so that the balance between fear and admiration does not topple. However, it is still possible to read the final draft and assume that the speaker is a figure living in the fallen world and deluded into thinking that his world is the real world—someone like Urizen as he appears in *The Four Zoas*, particularly in Night Seven (a), where he meets Orc:

> But Urizen silent descended to the Caves of Orc & saw
> A cavern'd Universe of flaming fire.
>
> [K320]

For in the final draft we find the assertion that the tiger may come from "distant deeps." To fallen man the tiger is horrific. It does not conform to established law, fails to fit into the established world picture, and is therefore evil. It is the corporeal eye of such a person that is described in *The Marriage of Heaven and Hell:* "The roaring of lions, the howling of wolves, the raging of the stormy sea, and the destructive sword, are portions of eternity, too great for the eye of man" (K151). /62/

But I think it is clear that there is, if not another speaker of the poem who presents us with an alternative reading, a higher imaginative level on which the poem must be read. On this level the speaker is the Blakean prophet himself, whose attitude casts an ironic perspective upon the words as they are spoken by our Urizenic questioner. This speaker knows the answers to his questions and is forming them rhetorically. This means ultimately that he is a visionary, a "mental traveller" who sees the world in its proper perspective. Careful examination shows that the questions he asks imply certain answers, and that from them we learn not only what the tiger is but also who his maker is. His attitude is thus opposed to the confused fear of the Urizenic questioner.

The question of stanza I involves the speaker's assumption that some "hand or eye" forms the tiger. The confused speaker cannot decide how the tiger was made. Was it the hand or eye of some all-powerful creator? In either case his interpretation is ominous. The physical creation of brute force is represented by the hand of God thrust down from above into our world. The creative eye suggests the capacity for wrath in God's imagination. The two possible gods, to this attitude, are thus the aloof deity of natural religion, who acts toward man as the speaker acts toward the poor fly in "The Fly," or the wrathful, avenging, spying deity of upside-down Christianity. A visionary perspective denies neither hand nor eye but casts them into a less ominous form and reads the "or" to mean "both" because the act of the hand is an extension of the eye's mental formulation. The hand is the shaping force of the blacksmith artist. The eye occurs elsewhere in Blake to suggest the shaping spirit of imagination. If we take the maker of the tiger to be God (provisionally, for he is a certain kind of god), the appearance of "eye" in this context means that God's method of creation is supernatural and that what He creates is not material. For Blake there is a clear distinction between the material, lidded or "outward" eye (an image like that of the "mundane shell") and the immortal, visionary eye which the artist sees *through* instead of with. The one raises a wall against true perception. The other opens a door: "If the doors of perception were cleansed everything would appear to man as it is, infinite" (K154). Erdman has pointed out that the eye appears as a visionary image in Blake's illustrations and drawings. In *Jerusalem*, Albion sleeps through history with eyes closed; his moments of vision and /63/ assertions of new life occur when he opens his real eyes and creates thereby the real world, not the nightmarish apparent one:

> Upon the Rock, he open'd his eyelids in pain, in pain he mov'd
> His stony members, he saw England. Ah! shall the Dead live again?
> [K742]

"Eye" suggests also the cycles of history named by God in *The Four Zoas* and *Jerusalem*. In those prophecies history is divided into seven (sometimes eight, depending upon whether Blake wants to include the apocalypse as the final eye) periods or "eyes of God," as Blake calls them. Each of these is a wheel containing within itself the microcosm of all history, each wheel the same play with different players; or perhaps better, each the same group of players acting a slightly different but archetypal drama: "as one age falls, another rises, different to mortal sight, but to immortals only the same . . . Accident ever varies, Substance can never suffer change nor decay" (K567). Thus each "eye of God" is an intuition of the full scope of the historic process, and the eighth eye will act as the culmination of this process. This view of history and reality is consistent with Blake's argument that reality lies within "minute particulars," if only each particular is observed *through* the eye. Thus each eye of God is figuratively the "world in a grain of sand." The tiger as a creation of the imaginative eye of God and a symbol of that imaginative power is microcosmically implicit in each cycle, immanent and imminent. To the tiger's more complex relation to the culmination of history or the "eighth eye of God," I shall return shortly.

The tiger-maker is not God, simply defined. He is a false god or the true God depending upon the speaker's perspective. Urizen would consider the maker of the tiger a false god, a devil—that is why Blake often sides with "the devil's party," as he seems to do in *The Marriage of Heaven and Hell*, showing that "angels" are representatives of passive reason and thus lieutenants of Urizen to be associated with the stars, while "devils" are truly creative: "Active Evil is better than Passive Good" (K77). Urizen's god is really the false god. Therefore, if the questions of the poem are taken as /64/ spoken by the materialist they imply fearfully that the creator of the tiger is some kind of interloper, a breaker of order. Icarus and Prometheus, the mythological personages of whom there are definite overtones in stanza 2, were both interlopers. Both defied the order of things (the material order, Blake would say) and both were punished for it. Icarus aspired to the sun and was flung down into the sea. Prometheus stole fire (the persistent image of Blake's poem) from the Gods, brought it to man, and was chained to a rock for his transgression.[3] There is a parallel to this in Blake's own work, where Orc, Blake's first major apocalyptic figure, is also chained to a rock so that he too may be controlled. According to Urizen, then, the creator of the tiger, a threatening figure like Orc, or perhaps Blake's ultimate hero Los, must be some lawbreaker sent by the forces of the devil himself. Part of Orc's serpent nature is imposed upon him by the deluded imaginations of Urizen.

But from the visionary perspective, the same questions are merely rhetorical. The same interlopers are not evil creatures but heroic representatives of energy. They have embarked on the inevitable journey any hero must make in order to meet the forces of materialism and to do battle with them. Icarus' ascent on wings attached to him by wax suggests a terrible misjudgment of the consequences of approach to the fire of heaven, but Prometheus' descent sets the stage for the more important final battle to come, the loss of Aeschylus' *Prometheus Unbound* being an irony of history. Prometheus' gift of fire to man symbolizes hope of eventual apocalypse, a cleansing of all material things in purgatorial flame. His act is therefore related closely to the image Blake draws of a burning tiger capable of causing a conflagration which will consume the forests. The

---

[3] Robert O. Bowen first mentioned these overtones in *Explicator*, VII, No. 8 (June, 1949), item 62.

"seizing" of fire is also the typical act of a blacksmith preparing to forge some object. In stanzas 3 and 4, furthermore, the speaker assumes that the creator of the tiger is a blacksmith. This particular smith is not only the strongest of creatures but also the greatest of artists. He is not only a Prometheus but also a Hephaestus; and we recall that the blacksmith Hephaestus was also hurled from heaven by Zeus, that he was the Greek god of fire, and that his name was used by Greek and Roman poets as a synonym for "fire."

From the perspective of Urizen again, the questions of stanzas 3 and 4 imply /65/ that the blacksmith is some devil-maker. If we take the blacksmith as an archetype of the artist, then we see that from this perspective the artist is a creator of illusions and that the poet, in Sir Philip Sidney's terms, "lyeth," but for evil reasons, not in behalf of active energy. Urizen would ban him from the republic for reasons somewhat different from Plato's—because he is a fabricator and a dangerous revolutionary who pretends to see a world other than the material one. In his annotations to Bacon's *Essays*, Blake objects to the idea of the poet's lying in order to give pleasure. Only someone who sees *with* the corporeal eye would for a moment be so naive as to say that the poet lies: "What Bacon calls Lies is Truth itself" (K397). Blake's blacksmith-artist Los works steadily with anvil and forge, hand and eye; the wonders of his labors are his creations of form out of miasma. His actions illustrate the principle of *outline* in Blake's aesthetic. According to Blake, when error is given proper outline it ceases to be error, for in its true form it has lost the power to delude. If, then, we begin to suspect that the creator of the tiger is, in Blake's terms, Urizen's nemesis Los, we shall not be far wrong.

But this is not the whole story either. Stanza 5 is perhaps the most difficult in the poem. No interpretation of it that I have seen seems adequate. The most elaborate recent one is by Kathleen Raine in an essay which proposes to find the answer to the poem's question (Who made the tiger?) in Blake's alchemical and occult reading.* She points to a quotation from Reuchlin's *De Arte Cabbalistica*, which is mentioned twice by Robert Fludd in his *Mosaicall Philosophy* and once by Thomas Vaughn in his *Lumine de Lumine*, "both books well-known to Blake." The quotation is: "There is not an herb here below but he hath a star in heaven above; the star strikes him with her beams and says to him: Grow." Miss Raine construes the action of the stars in throwing down their "spears" (beams) as making possible the creation or "growth" of the tiger and the fallen world. By a somewhat devious process of reasoning, Miss Raine concludes

---

* Kathleen Raine, "Who Made the Tyger?" *Encounter*, II, No. 6 (June, 1954), 43-50.

that the Elohim (whom she associates with Urizen), as distinct from God, created the tiger, because in Blake's sources the Elohim created the fallen world. Therefore, she argues, "the answer is beyond all possible doubt, No"; God, who created the lamb, did not create the tiger.

I can only say that I totally disagree with the conclusion and the method used to arrive at it. Miss Raine has perhaps discovered a valuable source for /66/ Blake's star imagery, but she has completely ignored what Blake has done with the imagery in assimilating it to the poem and has wrenched the poem out of Blake's own symbolic system. In the first place, if we accept the source, Blake has substituted "spears" for "beams," and it is difficult to assume that he did this merely to find a rime for "tears." "Spears" brings a suggestion of war into the poem. "Stars" in Blake's symbolism are always associated with Urizen and materialism. As warriors they seem to represent his own legions, who have lost the battle against the creator of the tiger and in the course of attempting to negate active energy have actually helped to create what they most feared—the wrath of righteousness. I believe that further examination of Blake's imagery here will sustain this view. In Blake's symbolism the stars represent the movement of a delusory scientific time and the concave, inner surface of the mundane egg, which is the fallen world. The image is particularly apt because the stars are ineffectual in daylight; they are apparent only at night or during fallen history. To Urizen the act of the stars in throwing down their spears would suggest the creation of the material world—the end of the "wars of Eden" leading to the fall. Stars are traditionally angelic intelligences, but Blake uses both angels and stars ironically as forces of reaction and passive good. The action of the stars here represents a fall in the war in heaven during which the "demonic" orders, represented by the tiger, were created. An important analogy to this act occurs in the Preludium to *Europe* already mentioned where the earth-female characterizes herself as an upside-down tree, the inverted delusory fallen sephirotic tree of the Cabala, and the stars that appear to be rising are in fact the fallen angels and false gods, while the falling stars are the rising gods. This topsy-turvyness is typical of Blake's fallen world and accounts for Urizen's loss of direction in *The Four Zoas*.

Several commentators upon this poem (most recently F. W. Bateson) have pointed out that the stars also throw down their spears in Night V of *The Four Zoas*. In this passage Urizen is speaking of past events:

"I well remember, for I heard the mild & holy voice
"Saying, 'O light, spring up & shine,' & I sprang up from the deep.
"He gave to me a silver scepter, & crown'd me with a golden crown,
"& said, 'Go forth & guide my Son who wanders on the ocean.'

"I went not forth: I hid myself in black clouds of my wrath;   /67/
"I call'd the stars around my feet in the night of councils dark;
"The stars threw down their spears & fled naked away.
"We fell. I siez'd thee, dark Urthona."

                      [K310-11]

This passage tells of a fall (obviously based on Milton's account of the Fall of the Angels, says Bateson) similar to that in *The Book of Urizen*, but here it is told not objectively but from Urizen's point of view. Here, too, we have a rather different Urizen, at least partially aware of the pathos of his fall. The stars are, in any case, the legions of Urizen now fallen into the upside-down material world of his own mental construction, a world created when Albion fell asleep:

But now the Starry Heavens are fled from the mighty limbs of Albion.
                      [K486]

They now compose the "starry floor" or the limit of the fall referred to in "Introduction" to *Songs of Experience*. Urizen's error is to think that they are rising points of light while the energetic light of, to him, the demonic orders is destined for some awful abyss. The stars are trapped, then, in the world delusion which Urizen next proposes to explore:

"I will arise, Explore these dens, & find that deep pulsation
"That shakes my cavern with strong shudders; perhaps this is the night
"Of Prophecy, & Luvah hath burst his way from Enitharmon.

                      [K311]

Urizen's song ends with his proposing to organize his domain, the materialist world. It is unlikely that in the stubbornness of his own revolt Urizen (if we may conjecture) would fully understand the weeping of the stars. He might consider it an expression of pity for those hurt in the havoc wrought by his "necessary" war in behalf of progress. But it is more likely that the tears are really tears of chagrin and fear reminiscent of the allegory in Blake's *America*, in which the soldiers of the king of England, also associated with Urizen, throw down their arms to flee the vision of revolt, Orc.[4] Urizen would not /68/ understand the chagrin of the stars at their woeful upside-down enclosure in the "starry floor" of circular zodiacal movement—for him this would constitute the brilliant new order:

---

[4] See Erdman, pp. 178-79; also Mark Schorer, *William Blake, The Politics of Vision* (New York: Holt, 1946), p. 251: "When the stars throw down their spears and weep, they are soldiers abandoning their arms in contrition and readiness for peace."

In sevens & tens & fifties, hundreds, thousands, number'd all
According to their various powers, subordinate to Urizen
And to his sons in their degrees & to his beauteous daughters,
Travelling in silent majesty along their order'd ways
In right lined paths outmeasur'd by proportions of number, weight,
And measure, mathematic motion wondrous along the deep.

[K287]

These lines are from a section of *The Four Zoas* in which we see Urizen's ordered world as Urizen may first have seen it in the flush of creative pride.

From the point of view of the visionary, the action of the stars is more profound. As Erdman suggests:

> The climax of the forging [of stanza 4 of "The Tyger"] is a mighty hammering which drives out the impurities in a shower of sparks, like the falling stars children call angels' tears. At this point in "The Tyger" Blake employs the symbols which in his political writing signify the day of repentance when the king's "starry hosts" shall "throw down . . . sword and musket."[5]

For the visionary the image of these lines leads toward an intuition of apocalypse when, with the tiger formed, the sparks hurled, and heaven itself cleansed by pity and (perhaps, ironically) by fear, total resolution can be foreseen. The imagery of the stanza, rather than deriving its meaning from a single source, seems to me to describe an ambiguous event. If Miss Raine's hint is useful, it is to suggest that the hurling down of the spears of light at the time of the creation of the tiger is one of those typically ambiguous Blakean acts in which progression comes out of its own opposite. Thus the capitulation of the stars, in contributing to the "growth" of the fallen world, helps to bring about its apocalyptic destruction, just as Los's "hand or eye" brings form out of miasma and completes a divine plan which seems to have begun in total degradation. /69/ The visionary understands the paradox of progress and therefore is able to "keep the divine vision in time of trouble." The falling of the stars into the "starry floor" of the heavens is combined, then, with an image of pity, for they fall into this position in the form of tears, where they are a constant reminder of God's mercy in creating a lower limit for the fall.

There is a further qualification to be made. For Blake, there are true and false tears, true and false pity. For someone like Los, the true pity is

---

5 Ralph D. Eberly has also associated the spears with a shower of sparks from a heavenly smithy; see *Explicator*, VIII, No. 2 (November, 1949), 12.

to hold in check any immediate or sentimental expression of that emotion, just as Orc in Night VII of *The Four Zoas* "contemns" the pity of Urizen (K322). If Los were to pity Urizen before he had given him his true form, he would harm the whole of creation in the long run. Los, as artist, must purge himself even of apparent pity in order to be capable of its higher form. The violent tiger itself is Blake's symbol for the denial of false pity. Urizen was fooled by the stars; they pitied themselves. The kind of pity of which Urizen is capable in his fallen state is itself error. When Blake speaks of Satan as having no "science of wrath, but only of pity" (K490), he indicates the necessity of one contrary paradoxically assisting the creativity of the other. Only Los marries the contraries.

In the fallen world even the apocalypse seems to have an ambiguous form. In total resolution the purgation by flame which is the tiger and the baptism by tears which is the weeping of the stars lead out of the fallen world into the new in the traditional rituals of rebirth. The balance of contraries is achieved, and the tiger lies down with the lamb, an image to which Blake turns in other lyrics.

If by now we do not have a fairly clear idea of who created the tiger and what the tiger is, the prophetic books can tell us more. In stanza 2 the word "dare" dramatically replaces the word "could" of stanza I. Physical strength to create the tiger is evidently not the only necessity—there must be *will;* the figurative journey is both physically and spiritually difficult. In the prophecies the tenacious spirit is Los, who wipes "the sweat from his red brow" and confronts those miasmal, hovering, indefinite creatures to whom he must give a /70/ form. It is Los, then, who howls in anguish, bestows no false pity, and holds to his task:

> I know that Albion has divided me, and that thou, O my Spectre,
> Hast just cause to be irritated; but look stedfastly upon me;
> Comfort thyself in my strength; the time will arrive
> When all Albion's injuries shall cease.
>
> [K626]

If we return for a moment to a point already made about Blake's theory of vision, we recall that he found the visionary at least latent in every man. Every man is a Los or at least has a Los. When in *Milton* Blake finds his own prophetic inspiration, it is Los who appears to him as a burning spiritual form:

> . . . Los descended to me:
> And Los behind me stood, a terrible flaming Sun, just close

Behind my back. I turned round in terror, and behold!
Los stood in that fierce glowing fire, & he also stoop'd down
And bound my sandals on in Udan-Adan; trembling I stood
Exceedingly with fear & terror, standing in the Vale
Of Lambeth; but he kissed me and wish'd me health,
And I became One Man with him arising in my strength.
'Twas too late now to recede. Los had enter'd into my soul:
His terrors now posses'd me whole! I arose in fury & strength.

[K505]

Since the power of vision is the power of artistic creation in a nonmaterial world, the power of God is the power of man, and each man is a kind of artist. It is no surprise to see that Blake takes the next step and asserts that man is a microcosm of God, God is the spiritual body of communal man.

In *Jerusalem*, when the seven eyes of God are named, it is said that "they nam'd the Eighth: he came not, he hid in Albion's Forests" (K686). For fallen man, such a creature is truly horrendous, hidden gleaming like an eye—like a tiger—in darkness, an image of the judgment he fears. Fallen man sees with "a little narrow orb, clos'd up & dark / Scarcely beholding the great light" (K484). Such an eye, Blake implies, cannot "judge of the stars" and /71/ can therefore certainly "measure the sunny rays" (K485).[6] For such an eye, tigers and lions are not human forms but those "dishumaniz'd men" (K314) seen by Urizen in his travels. Their spiritual reality is covered over by a material excrescence:

... A Rock, a Cloud, a Mountain,
Were now not Vocal as in Climes of happy Eternity
Where the lamb replies to the infant voice, & the lion to the man of years
Giving them sweet instructions; where the Cloud, the River & the Field
Talk with the husbandman & shepherd.

[K315]

But for the visionary, the tiger illuminated is the tiger creating out of the forest the light of day in one vast apocalyptic conflagration similar to the awakening of Albion in *Jerusalem:*

... Albion rose
In anger, the wrath of God breaking, bright flaming on all sides around
His awful limbs; into the Heavens he walked, clothed in flames.

[K742]

---

[6]Compare the angel in *The Marriage of Heaven and Hell,* whose fear makes him see hell in the form of a gigantic serpent with a forehead colored like that of a tiger, while Blake sits beside a bank listening to a harpist. For the political implications of the passage see Erdman, p. 165.

The leap of the tiger in the forest, inevitable to the eye of the visionary, is equivalent to the purgative fire which sweeps all before it, the eighth eye of God rending the veil of materialism. The tiger is thus an image of man's own hopes—the God in man, but also something created by the artist in man on the anvil of inspiration. It is a "fearful" image because, in the "forests of the night," false pity is misdirected. The artist who chooses to capture the miasmal mist of error and from it create significant form must not succumb to the temptations of right reason: "The tygers of wrath are wiser than the horses of instruction" (K152). To do so would be suddenly to succumb to the Urizenic view of what the tiger represents. Blake, himself, knew the temptation to treat the tiger as an obsessive, evil demon: "I am under the direction of Messengers from Heaven, Daily & Nightly; but the nature of such things is not, as some /72/ suppose, without trouble or care. Temptations are on the right hand & left; behind, the sea of time & space roars & follows swiftly: he who keeps not right onward is lost, & if our footsteps slide in clay, how can we do otherwise than fear & tremble" (K812-13). And even Los is capable of momentary delusion during which the negative hatred of the spectre appears similar to the tiger's wrath:

> While Los spoke the terrible Spectre fell shudd'ring before him,
> Watching his time with glowing eyes to leap upon his prey.
>
> [K627]

But in certain visionary circumstances wrath and pity merge in a single imaginative act. The totality of the man of imagination, expressed in the image of the four Zoas and their eyes is combined with the seven lamps, the seven spirits, and the seven seals of Revelation in Blake's description of his pictorial *Vision of the Last Judgment:* "The whole upper part of the Design is a view of Heaven opened: around the Throne of Christ [in a cloud which rolls away are the] Four Living Creatures filled with Eyes, attended by Seven Angels with the Seven Vials of the Wrath of God" (K444). Blake clearly associates these seven angels and vials with his own seven historical cycles culminating in the total eighth.

The eighth eye or total man is the "Four Living Creatures." Even in his fallen state the prophetic power in this man is capable of being raised above his own sleeping form so that he may see God's wrath and its sevenfold cyclical expression in history as a form of spiritual recreation and therefore proper pity. This is the case with Milton:

> The Seven Angels of the Presence wept over Milton's Shadow.
> As when a man dreams he reflects not that his body sleeps,
> Else he would wake, so seem'd he entering his Shadow: but

With him the Spirits of the Seven Angels of the Presence
Entering, they gave him still perceptions of his Sleeping Body
Which now arose and walk'd with them in Eden, as an Eighth
Image Divine tho' darken'd and tho' walking as one walks
In sleep, and the Seven comforted and supported him.

[K496]

/73/

To "dare frame" the tiger's "fearful symmetry" is to "keep right
onward," to hold the visionary attitude. It is also to confront the tiger
with assurance. To be tempted and to succumb is to become the materialist
and to find oneself staring into a mirror at one's own spectre, without
realizing that one sees there the reflection of a brute self. Nature's
"vegetable glass" shows Urizen only his own image. Not knowing that he
sees himself, he chases that image through the world, failing ever to subdue
it. The "wild beast" which Blake calls the "spectre" in "My Spectre around
me . . ." is an intimation of the divided state of fallen man. If it is horrific,
its existence, like that of the tiger, indicates man's condition if he cares to
or can read the sign. In the conclusion of *Visions of the Daughters of
Albion*, Oothoon, a free spirit condemned as a harlot by the man she has
loved, lists a "glowing tyger" as one of the creatures of the night which
can be blotted out by the "mild beams" of the sun—beams which bring
expansion to the "eye of pity" (K195). Having come this far, Oothoon
needs only to see a little farther through the eye and into the tiger's fire to
understand that the blotting out of the horrific glowing tiger in the greater
light of the sun is similar to the disappearance of the sun in the light of
the glory of God, which is described to us in Revelation. In the apocalypse
the tiger's fire returns to the light of which it is fallen intimation. To the
visionary, the tiger symbolizes the primal spiritual energy which may bring
form out of chaos and unite man with that part of his own being which he
has allowed somehow to sleepwalk into the dreadful forests of material
darkness. In *Europe*, Blake speaks of materialist "thought" as the cause of
such a retreat from reality:

Thought chang'd the infinite to a serpent, that which pitieth
To a devouring flame; and man fled from its face and hid
In forests of night.

[K241]

The tiger is formed on the anvil of inspiration, which is the eye of man
and God, but it is also a symbol of the very same eye that created it, for
Blake believed that men are what they behold, that the outer and inner

worlds are really one: "To the Eyes of the Man of Imagination, Nature is
Imagination itself. As a Man is, So he Sees. As the Eye is formed, such are
its Powers" /74/ (K793). Several times in the prophetic books Blake
announces that a character has "become what he beheld." The manner in
which one beholds the tiger is all important to its and one's own spiritual
nature. As guardian of the forest it may either opaquely repel or indicate
the existence somewhere nearby of a gate into the state of vision. Man has
the power to create his world, for that world is really himself, caught in
the vortex where the spirit takes on perceivable form.

"The Tyger" is concerned with both the unprolific or distorting and the
truly creative process in spiritual life. The latter is a process equivalent to
the process of creation in art. Creation in art is for Blake the renewal of
visionary truth. From the point of view of the visionary, the tiger, fearful
as he may be, is created form, error solidified and metamorphosed into a
vision of the last judgment. He is, therefore, a creature to be confronted
and contemplated not with undiluted fear but with that strange gaiety
suggested by the visionary intensity of the poem itself—a gaiety which can
find a place in the divine plan for both the tears and spears of the stars,
for both Los and Urizen, and for both the tiger and the lamb.

E. D. Hirsch, Jr.

The Tyger*

This greatest of Blake's poems displays his most distinctive characteristic as a lyric poet: the contrast between his vividly simple language and his immense complexity of meaning. If this is a richer poem than "The Lamb," it is not because its language is more difficult. Verbally, the most daring phrase of "The Tyger" is "forests of the night," which is not different in kind from "clothing of delight" in "The Lamb." The great distinguishing mark of "The Tyger" is the complexity of its thought and tone.

Like "The Lamb," which it satirizes, it begins with a question about the Creator:

Little Lamb, who made thee?   Tyger, Tyger! burning bright
Dost thou know who made thee?   In the forests of the night
Gave thee life, & bid thee feed   What immortal hand or eye
By the stream & o'er the mead?   Could frame thy fearful symmetry?

While "The Lamb" answers the questions it poses, "The Tyger" consists entirely of unanswered questions. In this simple fact lodges much of the poem's richness. The questions it asks are ultimate ones, and while the answers are implicit in the poem, they cannot be pat answers because, no matter how the reader construes its implications, the poem remains a series of questions. The way each question is formed makes it also an answer, but /245/ still the answer is formed as a question, and neither is resolved into the other. All the complexities of the poem are built on this doubleness in its rhetoric, and every aspect of the poem partakes of this doubleness.

---

* Reprinted from *Innocence and Experience: An Introduction to Blake* (New Haven: Yale University Press, 1964), pp. 244-252, by permission of the publisher.

Blake's first intention in forming such a poem was no doubt to satirize the singlemindedness of "The Lamb," a poem which excluded all genuine terror from life and found value only in what is gentle, selfless, pious, and loving. It is true that the *Songs of Innocence* as a whole do not exclude cruelty and terror. In "Night," "wolves and tygers howl for prey," and in other poems there is a sufficiency of pain and tears. But cruelty and terror are presented as aspects of life that are to be finally overcome and therefore have no permanent reality or value. In "Night" the lion is ultimately transformed into a loving guardian; in Eternity he lies down with the lamb. Thus, while *Innocence* acknowledges tigerness, it entertains two reassuring ideas about it: that it is temporary and transcended, and that it is directly opposite to true holiness, which consists entirely of the lamblike virtues of Mercy, Pity, Peace, and Love. These are the two ideas that "The Tyger" satirizes as illusions. To the idea that the terrors of life will be transcended, the poem opposes a tiger that will *never* lie down with the lamb. He is just as fundamental and eternal as the lamb is. To the idea that only lamblike virtues are holy, the poem opposes a God who is just as violent and fiery as the tiger himself. He is not a God whose attributes are the human form divine, but a God who is fiercely indifferent to man. Thus, to the singlemindedness of "The Lamb," "The Tyger" opposes a double perspective that acknowledges both the human values of Mercy, Pity, and Love, and, at the same time, the transhuman values of cruelty, energy, and destructiveness.

For this reason "The Tyger," is not primarily a satirical poem. It submerges its satire beneath its larger con- /246/ cerns. It counters "The Lamb" by embracing both the lamb and the tiger, and it accomplishes this by embracing two attitudes at once. That is the brilliant service performed by the device of the question. The first stanza, for example, really makes two statements at once. The speaker's incredulity when confronted by a tiger who is just as fundamental as a lamb is the incredulity of one who is still close to the standpoint of *Innocence*. Could *God* have made this ferocity? Is there, after all, radical evil in the world? Can it be that the God who made the tiger is a tiger-God? The speaker's astonishment is that of a man who confronts for the first time the possibility that what is divine may not be what is reassuring in terms of human values, may indeed be entirely evil from the exclusively human perspective. All sympathetic readers of the poem have experienced this evocation of an evil that in human terms remains evil. Blake meant us to experience this, as we know from such phrases in the first draft as "cruel fire," "horrid ribs," and "sanguine woe."

Nevertheless, Blake canceled these phrases because they interfered with an equally powerful affirmative motif in the poem. This is easily seen when

the moral astonishment of the question is transformed into something quite
different by converting the question to a statement:

> Tyger, Tyger burning bright
> In the forests of the night
> None but immortal hand or eye
> Could frame thy fearful symmetry.

That would simplify the poem quite as much as "horrid ribs" and
"sanguine woe," but it would also show that the *language* of the poem
makes an affirmation that is just as powerful as its horrified confrontation
of radical evil. /247/

That is because the tiger is not simply burning; he is burning bright. His
ferocity and destructiveness are not diminished by his brightness, but
transfigured by it. His world is the night—dangerous, and deadly—but
"forests," like "bright" transfigures all that dread. Blake's usual word for a
tiger's habitat was "desart" ("The Little Girl Lost") and it was the word
normally used by Blake's contemporaries, if we may judge from Charles
Lamb's misquotation of the line: "In the desarts of the night."[1] "Forests,"
on the other hand, suggests tall straight forms, a world that for all its
terror has the orderliness of the tiger's stripes or Blake's perfectly balanced
verses. The phrase for such an animal and such a world is "fearful
symmetry," and it would be a critical error to give preponderance either to
that terror or that beauty.

Nor should we regard the image summoned up by the incantation of the
first line as anything less than a symbol of all that is dreadful in the world.
For the terror of the vision corresponds to the terror of the created thing
itself—the *felis tigris*. No other animal combines so much beauty with so
much terror. The symbol of the natural fact is grounded in the natural
fact. The speaker's terror thus constitutes an insight that is just as
profound as the poet's admiration of the tiger's beauty, and to disregard
that terror is to trivialize the poem. "The Tyger" is not about two modes
of looking at a tiger but about the nature of the creation. /248/

In the "Proverbs of Hell," Blake had celebrated the divinity of natural
strife and energy, and in the revision of *There Is No Natural Religion* he

---

[1] See Lamb's letter to Barton, May 15, 1824: "Blake is a real name, I assure you, and
a most extraordinary man if he be still living. He is the Robert Blake whose wild designs
accompany a splendid folio edition of the 'Night Thoughts' . . . His poems have been
sold hitherto only in Manuscript. I never read them; but a friend at my desire procured
the 'Sweep Song.' There is one to a tiger which I have heard recited, beginning:

> Tiger, Tiger burning bright,
> Thro' the desarts of the night."

had stated quite unambiguously: "He who sees the Infinite in *all* things
sees God." There can be no doubt that "The Tyger" is, among other
things, a poem that celebrates the holiness of tigerness. This aspect of the
poem is reminiscent of one of the Proverbs of Hell: "The roaring of lions,
the howling of wolves, the raging of the stormy sea, and the destructive
sword, are portions of eternity too great for the eye of man." But the
poem is a far greater statement of this religious faith than the proverb,
because the mere assertion that the terrors of creation have a holiness
transcending the human perspective is too complacent to be believed. How
can this confident assertion be too great for the eye of man? Though the
raging of the sea may be holy, it is merely terrible to the man at sea,
unmitigably evil and malignant. Blake's accomplishment in "The Tyger" is
to preserve the divine perspective without relinquishing the human. The
union of terror with admiration makes the general tone of the poem that
of religious awe, but this general tone is compounded of two attitudes that
never altogether collapse into one another.

   In the second stanza, Blake continues to evoke the doubleness of the
tiger in images which suggest equally God and the Devil:

> In what distant deeps or skies
> Burnt the fire of thine eyes?

Is the tiger's fire from the deeps of Hell or the heights of Heaven? Whether
good or evil, the fire has a provenance beyond the realm where human
good or evil have any meaning.

> On what wings dare he aspire?
> What the hand dare seize the fire?   /249/

Did the immortal dare to fly like Satan through chaos? Did he dare like
Prometheus to bring the fire from Heaven?

   As the God begins to form the tiger, the immensity of his power takes
precedence over the daring of his exploit:

> And what shoulder and what art
> Could twist the sinews of thy heart?

The twisting shoulder of the god forms the twisting sinews of the tiger's
heart. This imaginative identification of the tiger and the god carries the
same kind of double-edged implication as the preceding images. The
identification of the tiger and his creator turns the god into a tiger: if that
shoulder could make that heart, what must be the heart of the god? The
divine artist plays with ferocity out of ferocity. Yet if the god is a tiger,

then the tiger is a god. The fire of those eyes is the spark of divinity. As the astonished and uncertain mind of the speaker shifts alternatively from god to tiger he lapses into an incoherent confusion that makes no literal sense (The couplet is an unassimilated vestige from an earlier draft) but makes good dramatic sense:

> And when that heart began to beat
> What dread hand and what dread feet?

Finally, the creation of the tiger is seen not as an act of ruthless physical daring and power but as an act of fiery craftsmanship in a fantastic smithy. This is Blake's favorite image for artistic creation, whether it be the creation of a tiger, a world, a religion, or a poem. The fiery forge is a place where incandescent energy and artistic control meet, just as they meet in the fearful symmetry of the tiger. As the rhythmic pulses of the /250/ verse fall like hammer blows, the speaker looks alternatively at the maker and the thing made, in an ecstasy of admiration and empty horror:

> What the hammer? What the chain?

[The hammer is wielded by the god, the chain is beaten by the hammer.]

> In what furnace was thy brain?
> What the anvil? What dread grasp
> Dare its deadly terrors clasp?

These staccato beats of controlled fury are succeeded by a stanza of immense calm that enormously widens the imaginative range of the poem. It is a highly compressed and difficult stanza, but it is perhaps the finest moment in Blake's poetry:

> When the stars threw down their spears,
> And water'd heaven with their tears,
> Did he smile his work to see?
> Did he who made the Lamb make thee?

The effect of the last two lines is to throw into clear relief the unresolved conflict between the divine perspective that has been implied all along in the poem, and the speaker's terrified and morally affronted perspective. The god smiles, the man cowers. (Of course, God smiled, and the answer to both questions is, "Yes!" The entire stanza is formed from traditional biblical and Miltonic imagery, and within that tradition, "God saw

everything that he had made and behold it was very good.") But while the
man cowers, he has a growing sense of the reason for God's smile. It could
be a satanic and sadistic smile, but it could also be the smile of the artist
who has forged the richest and most vital of possible worlds, a world that
contains both the tiger and the lamb. /251/

This broader perspective is introduced in the first two, highly
compressed, lines of the stanza. "When the stars threw down their spears"
is an allusion to the angelic fall as presented by Milton:[2]

> They astonisht all resistance lost,
> All courage, down their weapons dropt.
>   [*P.L.* VII. lines 1838f.]

The defeat of the rebellious angels is followed by their being cast into Hell,
which is followed in turn by the creation of the world. That moment of
the angelic defeat is therefore a decisive moment in the divine plan. The
fall of the angels is the prelude to the fall of man, and in the tradition it is
thus the prelude to the bringing of death into the world and all our woe.
This moment begins the catalogue of evil and cruelty that will include the
tiger. Yet the angelic fall was also "his work." To smile at that is to smile
at the tiger.

But why does Blake call the rebellious angels "stars"? His reason belongs
to the central conception of the poem, and it is given in the next line:
"And watered heaven with their tears." The defeat of the angels caused
them to weep tears, and these tears, left behind as they plummeted to Hell,
became what we now call the stars. The angels are named "stars"
proleptically to explain the name now given to their tears. The immediate
result of the angelic defeat was therefore the creation of the stars, just as
its indirect result was the creation of the world. No doubt, the God whose
"work" was the angelic fall is a terrible and inscrutable God, but however
terrible his work is, it is sanctified by vitality, order, and beauty. The stars
of night are part of the same awesome design as the forests of the night
and the fearful /252/ symmetry of the tiger. When, therefore, the poet
repeats the questions of the first stanza, it is with no less terror but with
increased awe. The question is no longer how *could* a god—physically and
morally—frame such *fearful* symmetry, but how *dare* God frame such
fearful symmetry. The last line now emphasizes the artistic daring inherent
in a creation that is incredibly rich, and terrifyingly beautiful, and is like
God himself beyond human good or evil.

---

[2] Blake recalled this image of the angelic fall in his later description of Urizen's Fall,
The Four Zoas, V, lines 220-25, K.310-11.

While "The Tyger" expresses a religious affirmation that is common to all of Blake's poetry in the 90s, it is the most comprehensive poem Blake produced in that period. Philosophically, of course, it is no more inclusive than "The Clod and the Pebble," *The Marriage,* or *The Book of Urizen,* but in tone it is the most inclusive poem Blake ever wrote. It celebrates the divinity and beauty of the creation and its transcendence of human good and evil without relinquishing the Keatsian awareness that "the miseries of the world Are misery." For all its brevity, its spiritual scope is immense.

The Design

To the right of the text is the trunk of a large tree. Below the text, Blake has drawn a tiger which some critics have found to be rather tame. Obviously these critics have consulted only the earlier issues or reproductions of them. In the opaquely colored later issues Blake's tiger is quite ferocious. It is only to be expected that a tiger colored with light watercolor washes will be less terrifying than an opaque tiger with yellow about the eyes and vigorous mottles of dark green, dark brown, and yellow. Furthermore, the expression on the tiger's face varies considerably from copy to copy. The line of the mouth in the lightly colored copies appears to be smiling. In the opaquely colored ones, where Blake could cover the lines etched on the plate, the mouth is snarling.

Philip Hobsbaum

A Rhetorical Question Answered: Blake's Tyger and Its Critics*

The Tyger is, in Kathleen Raine's felicitous phrase, a "grand incantation of rhetorical questions."[1] By definition, and in common English usage, rhetorical questions are those which do not demand an answer or, at least, which do not expect one. But several attempts have been made to supply answers to *The Tyger*. Such attempts have resulted in interpretations which often have amounted to a rewriting of the poem in the critics' own terms. The main difficulties that critics have found can be reduced to a single question—Who Made the Tiger? The answers that have been put forward are various. We shall take them in increasing degrees of antipathy to the Creator, whoever he was.

Stanley Gardner is the critic most favourably inclined towards him. He finds parallels between the Tiger's creation and the compulsion of the invisible spectre by Los in *Jerusalem* and also with his "riveting of Urizen's changes" in the Book of Urizen.[2] Mr. Gardner's main arguments are based on the prevalent forge-imagery of all three passages. His observation is convincing, but his conclusion is less acceptable. "Now, as we have seen, the one power that has dared to grasp the 'deadly terrors' of the tyger in the night is Innocence."[3] There are two main objections to this identification. Mr. Gardner has not shown any reasons for equating the prophetic Los with Innocence. And he has not shown from the poem itself how far Innocence may be taken to be the Creator. Too many steps are left out of his argument. It is true that Mr. Gardner does not go as far as some critics who actually claim that the Lamb created the Tiger! But he

---

* Reprinted from *Neophilologus*, XLVIII (May, 1964), 151-155, by permission.
[1] Kathleen Raine, Who Made the Tyger? Encounter, June 1954, p. 43.
[2] Stanley Gardner, Infinity on the Anvil (1954), p. 125.
[3] ibid.

does suggest that there is a kind of resolution in the final stanzas when the "Creator (is) no longer Los or Urizen but the God of Innocence."[4]

Hazard Adams has said that man's imagination created the Tiger; but asks who it was who created this imagination. He answers the question himself. "He who seized the fire is, of course, Prometheus who brings knowledge to man, and the tiger represents such knowledge or revelation."[5] Mr. Adams says that the subsequent images tell us that the Creator is a blacksmith. Therefore, like Mr. Gardner, he equates him with the Los of the Prophetic Books.[6] But he does not really agree with him, since Mr. Gardner sees Los as Innocence, not Prometheus. In other respects, Mr. Adams's reading is similar to that of Mr. Gardner, even to finding a resolution in the final stanzas. It may be faulted, too, in the same terms. The links between the rationalization and the poem will probably seem arbitrary to the reader. At least, they appear to have been forged by the imagination of the critic rather than that of the poet.

Unlike these two critics, David Erdman is as conscious of the Creator's wrath as of his softer qualities. He feels that "the creative blacksmith /152/ who seizes on the molten stuff of terror and shapes it into living form on the cosmic anvil must employ dread power as well as daring and art, but the dread, Blake hopes, will be sufficient unto the day."[7] Such an interpretation would construe the poem as defending a war of necessity. Mr. Erdman anticipates objections to his unduly political interpretation by saying that the poem speaks generally of what specifically was true of the French Revolution. Therefore the Creator of the Tiger is necessarily a fierce God, but only until the battles are won. And then the foes will "co-exist with the Lamb, the wrath of the Tiger having done its work."[8] Here, like Mr. Gardner, Mr. Erdman is assuming a sequence that cannot be shown to exist. Neither of them do anything to demonstrate the development in the argument of the poem which is assumed in their interpretations—both of which, in spite of their differences, turn on the idea of reconciliation.

F. W. Bateson would probably agree with Mr. Erdman that the Creator of the Tiger is both a God of Wrath and a God of Mercy. But he does not see these, as Mr. Erdman does, as succeeding each other. Rather, for him, they are co-existent. Mr. Bateson points out the parallels between *The Book of Urizen* and *The Tyger*, as Mr. Gardner does. But he is less inclined

---

[4] ibid.

[5] Hazard Adams, Blake and Yeats, The Contrary Vision (1955), p. 238.

[6] ibid.

[7] David V. Erdman, Blake, Prophet against Empire (1954), p. 180.

[8] ibid.

to take Los as the Spirit of Innocence. He regards him rather as the Spirit of Prophecy.[9] He feels, also, that the poem is a demonstration of the duality of God rather than a commitment of the poet to one view or the other.

Like Mr. Bateson, Professor Damon has split the Creator in the poem into duality. His terms, however, are more familiar—he speaks of God the Father and of Christ. He quotes Blake as saying that Christ was the only God and "God out of Christ is a consuming fire." From this, he deduces that God the Father created the Tiger as an instrument for "the Punishment of Sins."[10]

Certainly Professor Damon has a strong case—strong from within the poem. The Creator is there said to be immortal. And one idea in the poem which is indisputable is that he has made a creature of infinite savagery. But that is as far as an identification will go; and such an identification as Professor Damon's must necessarily rest on a preconceived idea of God the Father. The reader who conceives of him as a Judge rather than as a Tyrant will not find the identification so readily acceptable as Professor Damon does. It may be argued that Blake made some such identification himself in the conversation that Professor Damon quotes. But we require the poem, not Blake's own comments, to make what for many must be a difficult judgment. And the remarkable characteristic of the poem is that it makes no judgment at all. It does no more than imply, through its chain of rhetorical questions, that a judgment needs to be made.

Margaret Rudd says that the poet is unsure of himself as to who made the Tiger. "Despite his firm stand on the side of the Lamb of Christ, /153/ Blake is bewitched by the burning energy of evil and satanic nature which is contained in the image of the Tiger. And it is only an abstract law of Urizen which calls the Tiger, like sex, evil."[11]

But in the poem there is found to be no wavering between the poles of evil and good. The questions all follow one pattern—asking, in their different ways, who the Creator was. There is no choice implied, even in the questions. The assumption is that the Creator of the Tiger will be either good or evil. But this does not mean that the poet is deciding himself. The decision has been taken already. The questions are designed to find out what it is—and, at the same time, by questioning, to present the difficulty involved in making a judgment. Basically, of course, the problem is much the same as that of *Hear the Voice of the Bard.* In neither of these

---

[9] F. W. Bateson (editor) Selected Poems of William Blake (1957), p. 117.

[10] S. Foster Damon, William Blake, His Philosophy and Symbols (1924), p. 227.

[11] Margaret Rudd, The Divided Image (1953), p. 91

poems can the Creator be easily typified; and Blake does not make the mistake of wanting to try.

Miss Rudd raises the question of whether the abstract laws of Urizen would call this impulse of destruction, the Tiger, evil.[12] But the point is irrelevant once we realize that neither the Tiger nor his Creator are called evil in the poem.

Kathleen Raine, making this assumption, necessarily draws from it the conclusion that the Creator of the Tiger must be evil (because the Tiger is). She agreed with Professor Damon that the Son of God made the Lamb; but she deduces this from the poem, *The Lamb*, itself. "Blake is making a specific theological statement: that the Lamb and the child are made by God the Son who became incarnate as Jesus."[13]

> *Little Lamb, I'll tell thee.*
> *Little Lamb, I'll tell thee.*
> *He is called by thy name.*
> *For he calls himself a Lamb.*

Helped by the circumstance of the second stanza answering the first, Miss Raine is able to make her point in a brief paragraph. *The Tyger*, however, is a series of questions, none of which is answered. In the remaining four thousand words of her essay, Miss Raine quotes Mosheim, the Gnostics, Robert Fludd, Hermes Trismegistus and Berkeley. This is her way of demonstrating what could, if at all, be inferred only from the poem: the identity of the Creator of the Tiger. In her opinion, it is Urizen.

Miss Raine finds especially in Hermes' book *The Divine Pymander* a passage which certainly parallels in its repeated questions the form of *The Tyger*. This, however, is a form not unusual in hortatory literature. But Hermes, after all his questions concerning the creation of man, is not himself clear as to who the creator was—just as *The Tyger* itself leaves us in a state of "sublime doubt."[14] And all Miss Raine's quotations from sources other than the poem cannot assure us of Blake's intention in the poem. Only the poem can do that; and then, only if the intention is inescapably realized. But, when Miss Raine refers to the /154/ poem, it is in highly symbolic terms. "Never, to the best of my belief, is the word 'forest' used by Blake in any context in which it does not refer to the natural 'fallen' world."[15] This statement need mean no more than that the critic finds the poem's background detail appropriate. But Miss Raine goes on from this to

---

[12] ibid.

[13] Kathleen Raine, op. cit., p. 44.

[14] ibid.

[15] ibid.

an identification of the forest trees with the Tree of Life, and to an association of this with Urizen; and therefore, by analogy, with the Tiger itself. Such a conclusion is far-fetched. The links in the chain of association do not seem to have been observed by anyone other than Miss Raine herself. One may feel, too, that Miss Raine's procedure is too laborious to do much to prove her point. A statement like "Lamb and Tiger inhabit different worlds and are made by different creators,"[16] however it is backed up, must for its acceptance rest on the poem. And the poem never commits itself as definitely as that. In answering the poem's questions, Miss Raine is denying its *raison d'être*. She is seeking to resolve its "state of sublime doubt."

But Miss Raine is by no means alone in this. Consider the answers that have already been put forward. Some critics say that the Tiger was made by Los. But which Los? The Spirit of Innocence? The Spirit of Prophecy? Prometheus? Others say that it was made by God the Father. But which God the Father? A God of Wrath, a God of Mercy, or, as some say, both? And in the last instance, are the states of Wrath and Mercy co-existent or successive? Was the poet himself uncertain of his aim? Hardly; the poem is manifestly not a failure. Yet these interpretations do not merely vary; they flatly contradict each other.

It is quite evident that the critics are not trying to understand the poem at all. If they were, they would not attempt to answer its questions. The questions are there because the poet does not know the answer. In a sense, that is what the poem is about. It may be that there is no answer. Or that the answer is only to be defined in the questions which are asked. But whatever the answer is to the question, "Who Made the Tiger?", it is, by the terms in which the poem is couched, going outside relevant enquiry. The kind of answer the critics seem to be looking for could be another poem, a mystical treatise, a philosophical dissertation. It cannot be a critique.

It is possible to sum up by saying that, with very few exceptions, all critiques of this poem begin with a demonstrably just reaction to it. This could be shown by pointing to the general consensus of opinion about the Creator's courage and strength. Where the critics differ is when they come to rationalize the poem. Then they try to find answers for what it enacts. However, their attempt to answer Blake's rhetorical questions is a tribute to the force with which those questions are put. Blake gives us no chance to admire his 'beauty' or 'technique,' as less urgent poets do. There is nothing luxuriant about the poetry of Blake. For him it is, as it never is for the mere litterateur, a means of communication. We must applaud

---

[16] ibid., p. 48.

Blake for having driven his critics into reply /155/ rather than exegesis. However, one cannot help inferring that, in many instances, this eagerness to reply conceals disagreement which the critic is reluctant to admit, even to himself.

Morton D. Paley

Tyger of Wrath*

In peace there's nothing so becomes a man
As modest stillness and humility,
But when the blast of war blows in our ears,
Then imitate the action of the tiger:
Stiffen the sinews, summon up the blood,
Disguise fair nature with hard-favored rage;
Then lend the eye a terrible aspect:
Let it cry through the portage of the head
Like the brass cannon; let the brow o'erwhelm it
As fearfully as doth a galled rock
O'erhang and jutty his confounded base,
Swilled with the wild and wasteful ocean.
Henry V III.i.3-14

How would an ideal contemporary reader of Blake—one of those "Young Men of the New Age" whom he addressed in *Milton*—have regarded "The Tyger"? To such a reader certain aspects of the poem which modern critics have ignored would be obvious. In the rhetoric and imagery of the poem he would recognize an example of the sublime, appropriately Hebrew and terrifying. He would recollect analogues to the wrath of the Tyger in the Old Testament Prophets and in Revelation, and being an ideal reader, he would not need to be reminded that Blake elsewhere views the French Revolution as an eschatological event. He would also know that Blake characteristically thought of divine wrath as an expression of what Jakob Boehme calls the First Principle. His understanding of the poem would thus be affected by his connecting it with the sublime, the Bible,

* Reprinted by permission of the Modern Language Association from *PMLA*, LXXXI (1966), 540-551.

80

and Boehme. We later readers may also discover something about the meaning of "The Tyger" by considering it in relation to these traditions. That such an approach has something new and valuable to offer will be seen if we begin with what has previously been said about the poem.

I. "The Tyger" has always been one of Blake's most admired poems, and it was one of the few to gain even moderate notice in his lifetime. It was one of four Blake lyrics which were copied into Wordsworth's Commonplace Book in 1803 or 1804;[1] it gave Coleridge great pleasure;[2] Lamb thought it "glorious."[3] In 1806 it was printed along with a few of Blake's other lyrics in *A Father's Memoir of His Child* by Benjamin Heath Malkin.[4] It was one of five poems to appear in a German periodical in 1811, along with an article on Blake by Henry Crabb Robinson.[5] Allan Cunningham, in his *Lives of the Most Eminent British Painters, Sculptors, and Architects* (1830), said "The little poem called 'The Tiger' has been admired for the force and vigor of its thoughts by poets of high name."[6] Transcripts must have circulated privately: Damon says that "when the authentic text was published, protests appeared in various magazines, giving the lines 'to which we are accustomed'."[7]

The poem must have continued to pass from one friend to another after Blake's death (it was, of course, included in J. J. Garth Wilkinson's edition of the *Songs*, published in London in 1839), for Alexander Gilchrist, whose *Life of William Blake* appeared in 1863, wrote: "One poem in the *Songs of Experience* happens to have been quoted often enough . . . to have made its strange old Hebrew-like grandeur, its Oriental latitude yet force of eloquence, comparatively familiar:—*The Tiger.*"[8] The latter part of Gilchrist's statement echoes what Malkin had previously said: "It wears

---

[1] See F. W. Bateson, *Wordsworth, A Re-Interpretation* (London, 1954), p. 133; and *Selected Poems of William Blake* (New York, 1957), p. 116. Professor Bateson has informed me that the handwriting may be Dorothy Wordsworth's.

[2] See letter of 12 February 1818. *Collected Letters*, ed. Earl Leslie Griggs (Oxford, 1959), IV, 836-838.

[3] Letter of 15 May 1824. *The Letters of Charles Lamb & Mary Lamb*, ed. E. V. Lucas (New Haven, 1935), II, 424-427. For Blake's reputation among his contemporaries, see Geoffrey Keynes, "Blake with Lamb and His Circle," *Blake Studies* (London, 1949), pp. 84-104.

[4] London, 1806. The child, who died young, had been a drawing pupil of Blake's. Malkin's comment on "The Tyger" (see below) is slight, but his judicious remarks on some of the other poems entitle him to be considered the first Blake critic.

[5] See Arthur Symons, *William Blake* (London, 1907), pp. 278-279.

[6] Symons, p. 393.

[7] S. Foster Damon, *William Blake: His Philosophy and Symbols* (New York, 1947) [first published 1924], p. 276.

[8] London, I, 119.

that garb of grandeur, which the idea of the creation communicates to a mind of the higher order. Our bard, having brought the topic he descants on from warmer latitudes than his own, is justified in adopting an imagery, of almost oriental feature and complection."[9] By "Oriental" these writers mean Middle Eastern, Semitic; they recognize, however vaguely, that the poem has an Old Testament model, a fact of some importance to my own view of it.

But none of this so far amounts to interpretation, which begins with the first long critical /541/ essay devoted to Blake, Algernon Charles Swinburne's *William Blake*, first published in 1868. Although Swinburne's comments on "The Tyger" are scant, he does begin the long history of critics' attempts to determine its implications. I shall try to indicate what the important representative views have been.

Swinburne reads the poem as a piece of Romantic Satanism. Making use of Blake's Notebook, then in the possession of Dante Gabriel Rossetti, Swinburne prints an earlier version of the second stanza, then paraphrases it and some of the rest of the poem as follows:

> 'Burnt in distant deeps or skies
> The cruel fire of thine eyes?
> Could heart descend or wings aspire?
> What the hand dare seize the fire?'

Could God bring down his heart to the making of a thing so deadly and strong? or could any lesser daemonic force of nature take to itself wings and fly high enough to assume power equal to such a creation? Could spiritual force so far descend or material force so far aspire? Or, when the very stars, and all the armed children of heaven, the 'helmed cherubim' that guide and the 'sworded seraphim' that guard their several-planets, wept for pity and fear at sight of this new force of monstrous matter seen in the deepest night as a fire of menace to man—

> Did he smile his work to see?
> Did he who made the lamb make thee?[10]

By calling the Tyger a "new force of monstrous matter" and "a fire of menace to men," Swinburne distorts the question. He also ignores the typical meaning of stars in Blake's symbolism as well as the significance of

[9] *A Father's Memoir*, p. xxxvii.

[10] London, 1868, p. 120. For Blake's actual spelling and punctuation, see *The Complete Writings of William Blake*, ed. Geoffrey Keynes (London, 1966), pp. 172, 173, 214. This edition will hereafter be cited as K.

a cancelled stanza's being a cancelled stanza. Yeats and Ellis, editors of the first collection of Blake's complete works, take a different view in their brief comment: "The 'Tiger' is, of course, the tiger of wrath, wiser in his own way than the horses of instruction, but always, like the roaring of lions and the destructive sword, so terrible as to be a 'portion of eternity too great for the eye of man'."[11] S. Foster Damon, in his monumental *William Blake: His Philosophy and Symbols*, first published in 1924, finds the question of the poem to be "how to reconcile the Forgiveness of Sins (the Lamb) with the Punishment of Sins (The Tyger)." The Wrath of the Tyger had to be of divine origin ("His God was essentially personal; therefore Evil must be his Wrath"). The purpose of Wrath is "to consume Error, to annihilate these stubborn beliefs which cannot be removed by the tame 'horses of instruction'." Yet Damon also thinks that "Did he who made the Lamb make thee?" is "not an exclamation of wonder, but a very real question, whose answer Blake was not sure of."[12]

For Joseph H. Wicksteed, author of the most detailed commentary on the *Songs*, the poem's questions do seem to have a definite answer. "The whole thesis of 'The Tyger'," he writes, "is that he is a spiritual expression of the Creator himself . . . 'The Tyger' is a tremendous treatise enunciating the nature of the God that *does* exist—the God that is mightily and terribly visible in his creations." Attempting to discover the history of Blake's inner life through the visions and revisions of the Notebook, Wicksteed decided that "the composition of this great poem registers (perhaps effects) a change in Blake's mind," carrying him beyond the world view of the *Songs of Experience* to that of the prophecies.[13]

Since the time of these pioneer critics, writers on the poem have continued to disagree about whether the Tyger is "good," created by the Lamb's creator; ambiguous, its creator unknown and the question of the poem unanswerable; or "evil," created by some maleficent force. The first of these views has been given succinct expression by Mark Schorer:

> The juxtaposition of lamb and tiger points not merely to the opposition of innocence and experience, but to the resolution of the paradox they present. The innocent impulses of the lamb have been curbed by restraints, and the lamb has turned into something else, indeed into the tiger. Innocence is converted to experience. It does not rest there. Energy can be curbed but it cannot be destroyed, and

[11] Edwin John Ellis and William Butler Yeats, *The Works of William Blake* (London, 1893), II, 14.

[12] P. 277.

[13] *Blake's Innocence and Experience* (London, 1928), pp. 196, 212.

when it reaches the limits of its endurance, it bursts forth in
revolutionary wrath.[14]

Similar to Schorer's interpretation in this respect are those of David V.
Erdman, Stanley Gardner, Martin K. Nurmi, F. W. Bateson, and Martin
Price.[15] /542/

Among those who have seen the Tyger as either ambiguous or
ambivalent are Northrop Frye, Hazard Adams, Robert F. Gleckner, John E.
Grant, Paul Miner, E. D. Hirsch, Jr., and Philip Hobsbaum. Frye advises the
reader of the poem to "leave it a question." Adams, in his generally
valuable essay on "The Tyger," finds two views within the poem; however,
he emphasizes the "visionary" one, according to which "the tiger
symbolizes the primal spiritual energy which may bring form out of chaos
and unite man with that part of his own being which he has allowed
somehow to sleep-walk into the dreadful forests of material darkness."
Gleckner, setting "The Tyger" against some passages in *The Four Zoas*, also
finds two views. Grant, in his finely considered discussion, "The Art and
Argument of 'The Tyger'," indicates agreement with Wicksteed but, unlike
Wicksteed, finds only conditional answers.

> If he who made the Lamb also made the Tyger, it is because the two
> beasts are contraries . . . If the creator smiles because he sees that in
> the end the Tyger will leave the forest along with man, a man may
> feel justified in asking why it is his lot now to be cast among savage
> beasts. This question cannot be removed from 'The Tyger,' and, in
> spite of assertions to the contrary, it was one of the questions which
> continued to concern Blake throughout his life.

Both Miner and Hirsch find two different perspectives maintained
throughout the poem, though they see its final answer as affirmative.
Hobsbaum cautions readers against answering the questions, as he regards
Blake himself as being in doubt about them. [16]

---

14 *William Blake: The Politics of Vision* (New York, 1946), pp. 250-251.

15 Erdman, *Blake: Prophet Against Empire* (Princeton, 1954), pp. 179-180. Erdman,
like Schorer, regards the questions of the poem as rhetorical. Gardner, *Infinity on the
Anvil* (Oxford, 1954), pp. 123-130. Nurmi, "Blake's Revisions of *The Tyger*," *PMLA*,
LXXI (1956), 669-685. Bateson, *Selected Poems of William Blake*, pp. 117-119. Price,
To the Palace of Wisdom (Garden City, N.Y.), 1964, pp. 398-400.

16 Frye, "Blake After Two Centuries," *UTQ*, XXVII (1957), 12. Adams, *William
Blake: A Reading of the Shorter Poems* (Seattle, 1963), p. 73. Gleckner, *The Piper and
the Bard* (Detroit, 1959), pp. 275-290. Grant (ed.), *Discussions of William Blake*
(Boston, 1961), p. 75. Miner, " 'The Tyger': Genesis and Evolution in the Poetry of
William Blake," *Criticism*, IV (1962), 59-73. Hirsch, *Innocence and Experience: An
Introduction to Blake* (New Haven, 1964), pp. 244-252. Hobsbaum, "A Rhetorical
Question Answered: Blake's Tyger and Its Critics." *Neophilologus*, XLVIII (1964),
151-155.

Two recent commentators on the poem consider the Tyger to be perceived as evil. Harold Bloom regards this perception as the error of the "speaker" of the poem, which he thinks of as a monologue delivered by a Bard in the fallen state of Experience. "The Bard of Experience is in mental darkness ... The Bard is one of the Redeemed, capable of imaginative salvation, but before the poem ends he has worked his frenzy into the self-enclosure of the Elect Angels prostrate before a mystery entirely of his own creation."[17] This Bard, whom I cannot help regarding as entirely read into the poem, would resemble Adams' shadowy first speaker, for whom the creator of the Tyger must be a Urizenic God, a "devil-maker."[18] Miss Kathleen Raine, pursuing a different method, comes to a parallel conclusion: that the creator of the Tyger *is* such a devil-maker. She suggests sources in Gnostic and Hermetic mysticism as proof that "the Lamb was made by the son of God, the second person of the Trinity ... the Tiger was made by the demiurge, the third person of the (Gnostic and cabalistic) trinity. Lamb and Tiger inhabit different worlds and are the work of different creators." To Miss Raine the Tyger seems "a symbol of the competitive, predacious selfhood."[19]

The meaning of "The Tyger" has been and continues to be disputed. I would like to suggest that our understanding of the poem can be deepened and enhanced if we regard it against the traditions I have mentioned: that of Jakob Boehme, his predecessor Paracelsus, and his disciple William Law; and that of the British theoreticians of the sublime in the eighteenth century. These disparate traditions have at least one nexus other than their meeting in the mind of William Blake: for quite different reasons, the expression of the Wrath of God in the Bible, particularly in the Old Testament, is of great importance to each of them. This Biblical material also bears directly on Blake's theme in "The Tyger." I shall propose that "The Tyger" is an apostrophe to Wrath as a "sublime" phenomenon, to Wrath both in the Prophetic sense and as what Boehme calls the First Principle. The images and rhetoric of the poem will be found to support such an interpretation.

II. In the Old Testament Prophets, divine wrath is often associated with a Day of Yahweh which will accomplish the destruction of evil and establish a community of the righteous. In the later Prophets "that day" brings about a new earth and a new heaven, sometimes ruled by the

---

[17] *Blake's Apocalypse* (Garden City, N.Y., 1963), pp. 137-138.

[18] *William Blake,* p. 65.

[19] "Who Made the Tyger?" *Encounter,* II (1955), 48, 43.

Messiah. Similarly, the manifestation of wrath in Revelation destroys Babylon and is followed by the Parousia and the building of the new Jerusalem. This eschatological wrath, in both the Old and the New Testaments, frequently appears in the images of fire and of beasts of prey; sometimes it is represented by both together. Elsewhere, as the echoes of Isaiah in *The Marriage* and in *America* indicate, Blake portrayed the /543/ revolutionary events of his day as a fulfillment of this Prophetic vision. A few of many possible examples will suggest that he also did so in "The Tyger."

In the Prophets' depictions of the Day of Yahweh, the Wrath which brings on the establishment of the Kingdom is commonly depicted, as in Blake's poem, as fire:

> For, behold, the LORD will come with fire, and with his chariots like a whirlwind, to render his anger with fury, and his rebuke with flames of fire.
>
> (Isaiah lxvi.15)
>
> But who may abide the day of his coming? and who shall stand when he appeareth? for he is like a refiner's fire, and like fullers' soap.
>
> (Malachi iii.2)

Sometimes, once more as in Blake's poem, the image of a forest is introduced:

> Therefore, thus saith the Lord GOD; As the vine tree among the trees of the forest, which I have given to the fire for fuel, so will I give the inhabitants of Jerusalem. And I will set my face against them; they shall go out from one fire, and another fire shall devour them . . .
>
> (Ezekiel xv.6-7)
>
> But I will punish you according to the fruit of your doings, saith the LORD; and I will kindle a fire in the forest thereof, and it shall devour all things around about it.
>
> (Jeremiah xxi.14)[20]

In Amos, we find both the images of the beast of prey and the fire as symbols of God's wrath and coming Judgment:

---

[20] This passage from Jeremiah is cited in connection with "The Tyger" by Erdman, p. 181 n. A. J. Heschel writes in *The Prophets* (New York and Evanston, 1962, p. 116): "The divine word moved in Jeremiah as fire because he lived through the experience of divine wrath. Just as the pathetic wrath of God could become a physical fire of destruction, so the wrathful word of the prophet could work itself out as a destructive fiery element."

Will a lion roar in the forest, when he hath no prey?

(iii.4)

The lion hath roared, who will not fear? the Lord GOD hath spoken, who can but prophesy?

(iii.8)

Seek the LORD, and ye shall live; lest he break out like fire in the house of Joseph and devour it . . .

(v.6)

In beginning his poem with the Tyger burning bright in the night forests, Blake was using a figurative conception familiar to him in the writings of the Prophets. The allusion is to the Wrath of the Lord burning through the forests of a corrupt social order. To this eschatological conception Blake brings his own doctrine of contraries, partly derived from Boehme.

III. Jakob Boehme and his English disciple William Law occupy an important place in Blake's intellectual biography. "Any man of mechanical talents," Blake said in *The Marriage*, "may, from the writings of Paracelsus or Jacob Behmen, produce ten thousand volumes of equal value with Swedenborg's" (K. 158). "Paracelsus & Behmen appear'd to me," he wrote in describing his "lot in the Heavens" to John Flaxman (K. 799). Henry Crabb Robinson recalled that Blake called Boehme "a divinely inspired man." "Bl praised too the figures in Law's translin. as being very beautiful. Mich. Angelo cod. not have done better."[21] One of the seminal ideas that Blake derived from Boehme is that God manifests Himself in two contrary principles: Wrath and Love, Fire and Light, Father and Son. These principles are not dualistically opposed; they are contraries in an unending dialectic whose synthesis is the Godhead. As I think this conception is of great importance to an understanding of Blake's thought, I shall quote at some length from Boehme. Reference is to the "Law translation," which is really an edition made up by Law and his followers.

> As God the Father himself is *All*; he is the Number Three of the Deity; he is the Majesty; he is the still Eternity; he is the Nature, and in it he is the Love and the Anger: the Anger is a cause of his Strength and Might; as also a cause of Life, and of all Mobility, as the Poison [or Gall] in Man is: and the Love is a cause of the Heart of his Majesty, and a cause of the Number Three, and of the Three Principles.

---

[21] *Blake, Coleridge, Wordsworth, Lamb, Etc.*, ed. Edith J. Morley (Manchester and London, 1922), p. 6.

the Fire is a cause of the Light, for without fire there would be no Light, so there would be no *Love* without Light; the Light is Love . . . and we see that the Light and the fire have *two several* [properties or] sources; the *fire* is biting, wrathful, devouring and consuming; and the *Light* is pleasant, sweet, and desirous of a Body; the Love desireth a Body; and the fire also desireth a Body for its nourishment, but devoureth it quite; and the Light raiseth it up, and desireth to fill it; it taketh nothing away from the Body, but quickens it, and makes it friendly.

Thus we may consider with ourselves, *whence* it ariseth that there is a wrathful and a good will: For you see the Fire hath *two* Spirits, *one* is that which proceedeth from the Heat, and the other that which proceedeth from the Light: Now the Heat is Nature, and the Light is the Eternal Liberty without [or be- /544/ yond] Nature: for Nature comprehendeth not the Light.

And so you must understand us concerning the *two* sorts of wills in God, the *one* is Nature, and is not called God, and yet is God's, for he is angry, severe, sharp as a sting, consuming, attracting all things to himself, and devouring them, always striving, to fly up above the Light [which is the *other* will,] and yet cannot[22]

A flame represents the inter-action and interdependence of the two wills, its light corresponding to God's Love, its heat to His Wrath.

And yet the Fire gives or represents to us a *Mystery* of the eternal Nature, and of the Deity also, wherein a Man is to understand two Principles of a twofold Source, *viz.* I. a hot, fierce, astringent, bitter, anxious, consuming One in the Fire-source. And out of the Fire comes the II *viz.* the Light, which dwells in the Fire, but is not apprehended or laid hold on by the Fire; also it has another Source than the Fire has, which is *Meekness,* wherein there is a Desire of *Love,* where then, in the Love-desire, another Will is understood than that which the Fire has.[23]

Law is at least as explicit on the mutual dependence of the two wills and their ultimate unity:

the Father has his distinct manifestation in the fire, which is always generating the light; the Son has His distinct manifestation in the Light, which is always generated from the fire; the Holy Ghost has

---

[22] *The Threefold Life of Man,* Part 7, sections 62, 63, 65, 66. *The Works of Jacob Behmen, the Teutonic Theosopher* (London, 1764-81), II, 76.

[23] *Aurora,* Part 11, section 92, *Works of Jacob Behmen,* I, 99.

His manifestation in the spirit, that always proceeds from both, and is always united with them.[24]

Blake gave pictorial expression to the Two Principles in his allegorical illustration of James Hervey's *Meditations Among the Tombs*.[25] In one corner of the painting, to the left of God the Father, Blake wrote "Wrath"; in the other corner, "Mercy"; and directly to the left of God, "God out of Christ is a Consuming Fire." This again suggests that Blake characteristically thought of Wrath in Boehme's sense, for in *Aurora*, 14, No. 49, we find: "But in the Outspeaking of his Word, wherein the Nature of the spiritual World exists . . . and wherein *God calls himself an angry*, zealous or *jealous God and a consuming Fire*, therein . . . indeed God *has known the Evil* from Eternity . . . but therein is he *not called God*, but a consuming Fire."

The Two Principles are analogous to Blake's contrary states of Innocence and Experience. Meekness is apposite to the visionary poet in one State, Wrath in the other.[26] The poet of Experience must endeavor, like Boehme and Law, to show that Wrath is the self-executing judgment of God in a fallen world. By doing so, he will pass "beyond" Experience into inspired prophecy. The Tyger shows the way to this, embodying the Wrath of the First Principle unfolded in history as the great human upheaval of the French Revolution. Angels call it evil. The poet aspiring toward prophecy perceives and fixes its terrible energies as sublime.

IV. Terror, in the eighteenth century, was commonly considered the highest manifestation of sublimity. "Indeed," wrote Burke, "terror is in all cases whatsoever, either more openly or latently the ruling principle of the sublime." [27] Dennis had tried to explain why this was so.

the Care, which Nature has inrooted in all, of their own Preservation, is the Cause that Men are unavoidably terrify'd with any thing that threatens approaching Evil. 'Tis now our Business to shew how the Ideas of Serpents, Lions, Tygers, &c. were made by the Art of those

---

[24] "An Appeal," *Selected Mystical Writings of William Law*, ed. Stephen Hobhouse (New York, 1948), p. 46.

[25] The picture is reproduced in Damon's *A Blake Dictionary* (Providence, R.I., 1965), Pl. XI; Damon's interesting descriptive commentary is on pp. 183-184.

[26] I should note that Gerald E. Bentley, Jr., suggests, without going further into this subject, that "The question of 'The Tyger' is whether the wrath principle and the love principle emanate from the same eternal being."—"William Blake and the Alchemical Philosophers," diss. (Merton College, Oxford, 1954), p. 216.

[27] *Enquiry into the Origin of Our Ideas of the Sublime and Beautiful*, ed. J. T. Boulton (London, 1958), p. 58.

great Poets, to be terrible to their Readers, at the same time that we
are secure from their Objects.[28]

Burke's psychological explanation follows Dennis':

> Whatever is fitted in any sort to excite the ideas of pain, and danger,
> that is to say, whatever is in any sort terrible, or is conversant about
> terrible objects, or operates in a manner analogous to terror, is a
> source of the *sublime;* that is, it is productive of the strongest
> emotion which the mind is capable of feeling.[29]

The chief effect of the sublime is "astonishment"–"that state of the soul,
in which all its motions are suspended, with some degree of horror," and
"the mind is so entirely filled with its object, that it cannot entertain any
other, nor by consequence reason on that object which employs it" (p.
57). These effects are produced when we contemplate dangerous objects
which we know cannot /545/ harm us. Like Dennis, Burke finds examples
of this which bring Blake's poem to mind: "We have continually about us
animals of a strength that is considerable, but not pernicious. Amongst
these we never look for the sublime: it comes upon us in the gloomy
forest, and in the howling wilderness, in the form of the lion, the tiger, the
panther, or rhinoceros" (p.66).

For these writers the chief examples of the sublime in literature were to
be found in the Old Testament,[30] which they found particularly rich in
the sublime of terror:

> Now of all these Ideas none are so terrible as those which shew
> the Wrath and Vengeance of an angry God; for nothing is so
> wonderful in its Effects: and consequently the Images or Ideas of
> these Effects must carry a great deal of Terror with them, which we
> may see was *Longinus's* Opinion, by the Examples which he brings in
> his Chapter of the Sublimity of the Thoughts.[31]

Dennis goes on to produce examples of Wrath from Habbakuk and Psalms,
comparing them with passages from Homer to the advantage of the former
(pp. 366-368). Lowth writes, in a similar vein:

> Nothing, however, can be greater or more magnificent than the
> representation of anger and indignation, particularly when the Divine

---

[28] *The Grounds of Criticism in Poetry,* in *The Critical Works of John Dennis,* ed.
Edward Niles Hooker (Baltimore, Md., 1939), I, 362.

[29] *Enquiry,* p. 39.

[30] See Samuel H. Monk, *The Sublime: A Study of Critical Theories in XVIII-Century
England* (Ann Arbor, Mich., 1960), pp. 79-80.

[31] Dennis, *Grounds of Criticism,* p. 361.

wrath is displayed. Of this the whole of the prophetic Song of Moses affords an incomparable specimen [Cites Deut. xxxii. 40-42, followed by Is. lxiii.4-6] . . . The display of the fury and threats of the enemy, by which Moses finely exaggerates the horror of their unexpected ruin, is also wonderfully sublime. [Cites Ex. xv.9-10][32]

Of the Biblical passages which Dennis, Lowth, Burke, and others display as instances of the sublime, many have in common with Blake's poem the depiction of wrath in terms of fire, beasts of prey, or both. Lowth, for example, comments on

the sublimity of those passages . . . in which the image is taken from the roaring of a lion, the clamour of rustic labourers, and the rage of wild beasts:

JEHOVAH from on high shall roar,
And from his holy habitation shall he utter his voice;
He shall roar aloud against his resting-place,
A shout like that of the vintagers shall he give
Against all the inhabitants of the earth.

And I will be unto them as a lion;
As a leopard in the way will I watch them:
I will meet them as a bear bereaved of her whelps:
And I will rend the caul of their heart:
And there will I devour them as a lioness;
A beast of the field shall tear them.[33]

William Smith, in the notes to his translation of Longinus, gave a number of examples of sublimity, among them this passage from Psalm xviii: "There went up a smoke out of his nostrils, and fire out of his mouth devoured: coals were kindled at it . . . And he rode upon a Cherub, and did fly, and came flying upon the wings of the wind."[34] "The Sublime of the Bible," as Blake calls it in *Milton* (K. 480), was an established critical doctrine,[35] and the most powerful manifestations of such sublimity were in descriptions of divine wrath and power. The single book of the Bible which was considered most sublime in the eighteenth century, and which was also to be the subject of Blake's great pictorial interpretation in old

[32] Robert Lowth, *Lectures on the Sacred Poetry of the Hebrews* (London, 1787), I, 379-381.

[33] I, 363. Jer. xxv. 30, Hos. xiii. 7, 8. My own Biblical citations are from the Authorized Version, but in an instance such as this one where the author provides his own translation, I reproduce the text as he gives it, unless otherwise noted.

[34] *Dionysius Longinus on the Sublime* (London, 1743), p. 127.

[35] Cf. Coleridge's "Sublimity is Hebrew by birth," quoted by Monk, p. 79 n.

age, was Job. Lowth declared of the book as a whole: "Not only the force, the beauty, the sublimity of the sentiments are unrivalled; but such is the character of the diction in general, so vivid is the expression, so interesting the assemblage of objects, so close and connected the sentences, so animated and passionate the whole arrangement, that the Hebrew literature itself contains nothing more poetical" (I, 313). Almost all of Lowth's Lecture XIV, "Of the Sublime in General," is devoted to Job, in addition to three lectures on the work itself. Burke (p. 63) found Job iv. 13-17 "a passage amazingly sublime . . . principally due to the terrible uncertainty of the thing described." The same passage served Smith (p.152) as an example of the sublime of horror, and Blake used part of it as the theme for his ninth illustration to Job—"Then a Spirit passed before my face: the hair of my flesh stood up . . . Shall mortal Man be more just than God?" Section V of Burke's *Enquiry*, "Power," draws numerous examples of its subject from Job. Among these are the descriptions of Behemoth and Leviathan, symbolic beasts to which the Tyger is related as an embodiment of sublime power.

In his later writings and paintings, Blake portrays Leviathan as a demonic parody of the sub- /546/ lime, but this change in his symbolism, reflecting his changed view of revolution after the rise of Napoleon, occurred long after "The Tyger" was written. To ignore this fact in linking Tyger and Leviathan (as Bloom does, p. 138) is to distort the meaning of the poem. At this point we should rather think of the tiger-striped Leviathan of *The Marriage of Heaven and Hell*, which advances (from the direction of Paris)[36] "with all the fury of a spiritual existence" (K. 156). The Tyger is like the Leviathan of Job in that both are fiery images of divine energy:

> Out of his mouth go burning lamps, and sparks of fire leap out.
> Out of his nostrils goeth smoke, as out of a seething pot or caldron.
> His breath kindleth coals, and a flame goeth out of his mouth.
> In his neck remaineth strength, and sorrow is turned into joy before
> him.
>
> (xli.19-22)

Such power cannot be explained; it can only be evoked, as by the questions which the Lord asks Job from the whirlwind, or by those which Blake's speaker asks in "The Tyger."[37] "Did he who made the Lamb make thee?" no more demands an explicit answer than "Who hath divided a

---

36 See Nurmi, p. 671 n.

37 Erdman suggests a possible indirect connection between the two through a paraphrase in James Hervey's *Theron and Aspasio* (1775)—*Blake*, p. 103.

watercourse for the overflowing of the waters, or a way for the lightning of
thunder?" Leviathan is the culminating image of God's speech to Job
because as an embodiment of power it completes the process of raising the
Job problem out of the realm of ethical discourse, inducing an attitude of
awe, wonder, and astonishment which the eighteenth century called
sublime. This is the function of "The Tyger" in the *Songs of Experience.*

V.   The Tyger

> Tyger! Tyger! burning bright
> In the forests of the night,
> What immortal hand or eye
> Could frame thy fearful symmetry?
>
> In what distant deeps or skies
> Burnt the fire of thine eyes?
> On what wings dare he aspire?
> What the hand dare sieze the fire?
>
> And what shoulder, & what art
> Could twist the sinews of thy heart?
> And when thy heart began to beat,
> What dread hand? & what dread feet?
>
> What the hammer? what the chain?
> In what furnace was thy brain?
> What the anvil? what dread grasp
> Dare its deadly terrors clasp?
>
> When the stars threw down their spears,
> And water'd heaven with their tears,
> Did he smile his work to see?
> Did he who made the Lamb make thee?
>
> Tyger! Tyger! burning bright
> In the forests of the night,
> What immortal hand or eye
> Dare frame thy fearful symmetry?[38]

---

[38] K. 214. In one copy of the *Songs*, l. 12 was altered to "What dread hand Form'd
thy dread feet?" (Copy P, in Geoffrey Keynes and Edwin Wolf, *William Blake's
Illuminated Books: A Census*, New York, 1953, p. 61). Malkin printed the line as "What
dread hand forged thy dread feet?" Damon, *William Blake*, p. 279, thinks this
emendation was Blake's own. Bateson, *Selected Poems*, p. 118, notes that "forged" is
the reading in Wordsworth's Commonplace Book.

Our contemporary reader would have seen the sublimity of "The Tyger" not only in its theme but in its rhetoric and imagery as well. First there are the questions of which Blake's poem entirely consists, and which I have compared to those of Job: in both cases sublimity lies in the form as well as in the content. For example, Edward Young wrote in a note to his own verse paraphrase of Job: "Longinus has a chapter on interrogations, which shows that they contribute much to the sublime. This speech of the Almighty is made up of them."[39] Smith, commenting on that same chapter (xviii) in Longinus, remarked: "To these Instances may be added the whole 38th Chapter of Job; where we behold the Almighty Creater expostulating with his Creature. . . . There we see how vastly useful the Figure of Interrogation is, in giving us a lofty Idea of the Deity, whilst every Question awes us into Silence, and inspires a Sense of our own Insufficiency" (p. 155). Blake's poem has other sublime elements as well. Richard Hurd associated sublimity with "apostrophes and invocations"[40]—"The Tyger" is, of course, both. (Hurd also wrote that poetry "calls up infernal spectres to terrify, or brings down celestial natures to astonish, the imagination.") As for diction, Blake's exhibits the qualities which Lowth praised in Hebrew poetry—"sparing in words, concise, and energetic" (II, 250). One could easily apply to "The Tyger" the statement that "The sublimity /547/ of the matter is perfectly equalled by the unaffected energy of the style" (II, 251); Lowth is speaking of Psalm xxix, in which "The voice of the Lord divideth the flames of fire. The voice of the Lord shaketh the wilderness; the Lord shaketh the wilderness of Kadesh" (7-8, A.V.). Such a comparison was made more or less explicitly by Malkin, who in discussing Blake's *Songs* observed "The devotional pieces of the Hebrew bards are clothed in that simple language, to which Johnson with justice ascribes the character of sublimity" (p. xxxi). Among later writers on the poem, only Gilchrist made use of this hint. Also, in addition to being simple and energetic, Blake's diction employs what Professor Miles (p. 57) so aptly calls the "vocabulary of cosmic passion and sense impression" which characterizes the sublime poem of the late eighteenth century. Vistas open in "distant deeps or skies," penetrated by the "immortal hand or eye" of a being who dares "aspire" on "wings"; "the stars" and "heaven" participate in the cosmic drama. Other expressions, in stanzas three and four, belong to the vocabulary of the sublime of terror: "dread hand," "dread feet," "dread grasp," and "deadly terrors." In his use

---

[39] *The Works of Edward Young, D.D.* (London, 1813), II, 204. See also Lowth, I. 357.

[40] Quoted by Josephine Miles in *Eras and Modes in English Poetry* (Berkeley and Los Angeles, 1964), p. 66; from *On the Idea of Universal Poetry, The Works of Richard Hurd, D.D.* II (London, 1811), 9.

of sublime language, as Professor Miles has demonstrated, Blake is very much a poet of his era.

Having discussed the sublimity of "The Tyger," we must turn to the symbolic meanings which its images represent. It is here, of course, that Blake differs from poets who merely imitated the Bible. Blake's images have meanings which may in part be construed from the internal logic of the poem, but which also depend at least in part upon meanings established elsewhere, in Blake's other poems or in the traditional sources from which he drew. We learn to understand Blake's forests, tears, fire, stars, and furnaces as we do Shelley's veils, boats, rivers, and caves, or Yeats's spindles and swans. Meaning is affected by context, though not entirely determined by it. Fire, for example, has a different significance to Blake when it gives both heat and light than when it gives heat alone, and furnaces may be creative or destructive, depending on what is going on in them. In interpreting these images, we must beware of assigning sources too narrowly, or of mechanically transferring a meaning from one context to an entirely different one. We should, instead, try to understand what each image contributes to the effect of the poem as a whole.

The tyger embodies the *contrarium* of Wrath in the Godhead, "Burning bright" with Prophetic fire and perceived as a sublime phenomenon. He is God's judgment upon the world of Experience. In Blake's Notebook he appears after the moral terrain of that world has been charted in terms of the hapless soldier, the blackening church, the harlot, the chimney sweep. This debased and corrupt order produces a contrary to the Lamb of Innocence in the Tyger. But Contraries are not Negations. The Tyger is not "a symbol of competitive, predacious selfhood." Wrath is a vice only in the unfallen world of Innocence; in our world, in the London or Paris of 1792, Mercy and the other virtues of Innocence are vices.

> I heard an Angel singing
> When the day was springing,
> "Mercy, Pity, Peace
> "Is the world's release."
>
> Thus he sung all day
> Over the new mown hay,
> Till the sun went down
> And haycocks looked brown.
>
> I heard a Devil curse
> Over the heath & the furze
> "Mercy could be no more,
> "If there was nobody poor,

"And pity no more could be,
"If all were happy as we."
At his curse the sun went down,
And the heavens gave a frown.

And Miseries' increase
Is Mercy, Pity, Peace.[41]

The Tyger, ultimate product of Experience, shows the way out of Experience
to the earthly paradise of *The Marriage of Heaven and Hell:*

Then the perilous path was planted,
And a river and a spring
On every cliff and tomb,
And on the bleached bones
Red clay brought forth

But man's attempt to create such a paradise on earth came in the bloody
aspect of the French Revolution. "One might as well think of establishing a
republic of tigers in some forest of Africa,"[42] declared Sir Samuel Romilly
after the September Massacres, and Wordsworth in the fall of 1792 found
Revolutionary Paris /548/

a place of fear
Unfit for the repose which night requires,
Defenceless as a wood where Tygers roam.[43]

In *The Book of Ahania* (1795), where the energy principle temporarily
overthrows repressive reason, "Fuzon, his tygers unloosing, / Thought
Urizen slain by his wrath."[44] The image of the tiger seems to have been
almost inevitable.

Night, forests, and stars are frequently used by Blake as symbols of the
old order, *l'epaisse nuit gothique* of Holy Europe. "Thy nobles have
gather'd thy starry hosts round this rebellious city," declares the warlike
Burgundy to the King in *The French Revolution* (1791), "to rouze up the
ancient forests of Europe with clarions of cloud [loud?] breathing war" (ll.
100-101). He fears that the revolutionaries will "mow down all this great

---

[41] K. 164 ("Poems from the Note-Book 1793"). Deleted lines omitted.

[42] Quoted by Asa Briggs in *The Age of Improvement* (London, 1960), pp. 134-135.

[43] *The Prelude* (1805), ed. Ernest de Selincourt (Oxford, 1959), p. 370. For the date
of composition of "The Tyger" (fall of 1792), see Erdman, pp. 167 n. and 174; Nurmi,
p. 671 n.

[44] See my "Method and Meaning in Blake's *Book of Ahania,*" *BNYPL,*LXX (1966),
27-33.

starry harvest of six thousand years" (l. 90) and that "the ancient forests of chivalry" will be "hewn" (l. 93). In the same poem, Orleans, speaking for the popular cause, talks of "the wild raging millions, that wander in forests, and howl in law blasted wastes" (l. 227). This is similar, too, to "The Argument" of *The Marriage of Heaven and Hell*, where "the just man rages in the wilds / Where lions roam" (K. 149). In *Europe* (1794), "The night of Nature" is eighteen centuries of history which culminate in the war of 1793, when "The Tigers couch upon the prey & suck the ruddy tide" (K. 245). In the same poem man enmeshed in material error hides "In forests of night" (K. 241). There is, perhaps, a suggestion of Dante's *selva oscura* in the image, and of Spenser's Wood of Error. It may also recall Thomas Taylor's use of woods as a symbol of material nature,[45] and, as was pointed out earlier, the Prophets sometimes use the forest to stand for the corrupt order which God will burn. Blake need not have consciously borrowed his forest symbol from any of these sources to have been aware of its meanings in them. Such awareness, together with a feeling of affinity, influences the conceptions of a poet and makes traditional symbols viable in his work, as we see again in Blake's use of the stars.

Lines 17-18 have several related meanings. The literal image is of starlight and dew; Frederick Pottle suggests "When the stars faded out and the dew fell."[46] On the historical level, the stars represent the armies of monarchy; as early as the *Poetical Sketches* and as late as *Jerusalem*, Blake associates the stars with tyranny and war:

> The stars of heaven tremble; the roaring voice of war,
> the trumpet, calls to battle!
> "Prologue to King John," K. 34.

Loud the Sun & Moon rage in the conflict: loud the Stars
Shout in the night of battle, & their spears grow to their hands,
With blood weaving the deaths of the Mighty into a Tabernacle
For Rahab & Tirzah, till the Great Polypus of Generation covered the
Earth.   *Jerusalem*, 61: 31-34, K. 704.[47]

---

[45] "But when he [Virgil, in *Aeneid* VI] says that all the middle regions are covered with woods, this likewise plainly intimates a material nature . . ."—*The Eleusinian and Bacchic Mysteries* (New York, 1875), p. 20. See George Mills Harper, *The Neoplatonism of William Blake* (Chapel Hill, N.C., 1961), pp. 157 and 169.

[46] *Explicator*, VIII, No. 39.

[47] Cf. *Jerusalem*, 55: 27, where "The Stars in their courses fought," (K. 686), echoing Judges v. 20. Several lines after this, the Eternals name the Eighth Eye of God, but "he came not, he hid in Albion's Forests" (33). In this later phase of his thought, Blake believes that the destructive wrath of revolution should be restrained; therefore the Words of the Eternals are described as "Curbing their Tygers with golden bits & bridles of silver & ivory" (35).

"The stars threw down their spears" appears in Night V of *The Four Zoas*, where, as Erdman points out, Urizen's words refer to the defeat of the counter-revolutionary armies at Yorktown and Valmy:

> "I call'd the stars around my feet in the night of councils, dark;
> The stars threw down their spears and fled naked away.
> We fell . . ."[48]

(Also compare the defeat of the British as described in *America*, 15: 4-5: "The millions sent up a howl of anguish and threw off their hammer'd mail, / And cast their swords & spears to earth, & stood, a naked multitude.") The meaning of Blake's stars derives in part from Revelation. In xii.4 the stars are Satan's legions: "And his tail drew the third part of the stars of heaven, and did cast them to the earth"; while in the apocalypse of Chapter vi, after the Lamb of God opens the sixth seal, "the stars of heaven fell unto the earth, even as a fig tree casteth her untimely figs, when she is shaken of a mighty wind" (13). Coleridge, who like Blake saw the French Revolution as an apocalyptic event, uses this latter image in *Religious Musings:*

> And lo! the Great, the Rich, the Mighty Men,
> The Kings and the Chief Captains of the World, /549/
> With all that fixed on high like stars of Heaven
> Shot baleful influence, shall be cast to earth[49]

"This passage," Coleridge noted (p. 121), "alludes to the French Revolution. . . . I am convinced that the Babylon of the Apocalypse does not apply to Rome exclusively; but to the union of Religion with Power and Wealth, wherever it is found," a statement which could have been made by Blake as well. Revelation vi ends, significantly, "For the great day of his wrath is come; and who shall be able to stand?" (17).

Blake also thought of the stars as symbols of oppression because they were associated both with the mechanism of the Newtonian universe and with the instrumentality of fate. The defeat of the stars signifies the casting off of both cosmic and internal constraint, freeing man to realize his potentially divine nature. This is also a theme in Paracelsus and Boehme. Boehme wrote:

---

[48] K. 311. See Erdman, p. 178.

[49] Written in 1794. *The Poems of Samuel Taylor Coleridge,* ed. Ernest Hartley Coleridge (London, 1912), p. 121.

For *the outward life* is fallen quite under the power of the Stars, and
if thou wilt withstand them, thou must enter into God's will, and
then they are but as a shadow, and cannot bring that to effect which
they have in their power: *neither do they desire it*, but the Devil
only desireth it: For the whole Nature boweth itself before the will
of God: For the Image of God in Man is so powerful and mighty,
that when it wholly casteth itself into the will of God, it
overpowereth Nature, so that the Stars are *obedient* to it, and do
rejoice themselves in the Image: for their will is that they may be
freed from the vanity, and thus are kindled in Meekness in the Image,
at which the Heaven rejoiceth, and so the Anger of God in the
Government of this world is *quenched;* for when that is burning,
Man's wickedness is guilty of it, in that Men kindle it in the Spirit of
this world. (*Threefold Life*, Part II, section 38, *Works*, II, 116)

According to Paracelsus:

The stars are subject to the philosopher, they must follow him, and
not he them. Only the man who is still animal is governed, mastered,
compelled, and driven by the stars, so that he has no choice but to
follow them. . . But the reason for all this is that such a man does
not know himself and does not know how to use the energies hidden
in him, nor does he know that he carries the stars within himself, and
thus carries in him the whole firmament, with all its influences.[50]

After the failure of the Peasants' Revolts, Paracelsus declared: "The
peasants have submitted to the stars, and have been beaten by them.
Whoever trusts the stars, trusts a traitor."[51] In "The Tyger," the opposite
happens: the stars are beaten and desert their order. Man's fate suddenly
becomes of his own making, and the "just man" of "The Argument" can
create a human society, symbolized by the covering of the bleached bones
of the Old Adam with the red clay of the New.

The weeping stars of Blake's poem owe something perhaps to the
anonymous lyric "Tom of Bedlam," reprinted in Joseph Ritson's *Ancient
Songs* of 1790:

> I behold the stars
> At mortal wars,
> In the wounded welkin weeping

---

[50] *Selected Writings*, ed. Jolande Jacobi (New York, 1958), p. 154.

[51] Quoted in Henry M. Pachter, *Paracelsus: Magic Into Science* (New York, 1957), p.
107.

The tears in Blake's poem are doubtless the "tears such as Angels weep" in *Paradise Lost* I. 620,[52] but of Angels in the Blakean sense—they are tears of frustration, hypocrisy, repression. This is the burden of meaning carried by tears in other *Songs of Experience.* In "The Human Abstract," Cruelty "waters the ground with tears" in order to make the Tree of Mystery grow. The speaker of "The Angel" (K. 213-214) uses tears as a defense against feeling:

> And I wept both night and day,
> And he wip'd my tears away,
> And I wept both day and night,
> And hid from him my heart's delight.
>
> So he took his wings and fled;
> Then the morn blush'd rosy red;
> I dried my tears, & arm'd my fears
> With ten thousand shields and spears.

In the Lambeth prophecies, Urizen is often depicted as weeping because life cannot keep his iron laws. "And he wept & he called it Pity, / And his tears flowed down on the winds" (*Book of Urizen*, K. 235). Pity, as I have said, is a vice in the world of Experience. It is the error of La Fayette in the poem Blake wrote about him not long after "The Tyger":

> Fayette beheld the King & Queen
> In curses & iron bound;
> But mute Fayette wept tear for tear,
> And guarded them around.
>
> (K. 186)

Erdman suggests a parallel to this in Paine's condemnation of Burke's pity for Marie Antoinette—"He pities the plumage, but forgets the dying bird."[53] If the just man is to find his way out of /550/ the forest around him, he must give over his modest stillness and humility and imitate the action of the tiger.

Having discussed the tiger-fire images in the poem and the stars-forest-tears constellation, we must now turn to the third important group of images, those concerned with metalworking.

---

[52] *The Works of John Milton,* ed. Frank Allen Patterson (New York, 1931), II, i, 30.
[53] P. 168, from *Rights of Man* (London, 1791), 4th ed., p. 26.

> What the hammer? what the chain?
> In what furnace was thy brain?
> What the anvil? what dread grasp
> Dare its deadly terrors clasp?

These instruments—hammer, chain, furnace, and anvil—are in Blake's prophetic writings assigned to Los, Eternal Prophet, and symbol of the Imagination.[54] It is the function of Los to create the imaginative constructs which give form to human perception. On plate 6 of *Jerusalem* he is pictured with all four instruments mentioned in "The Tyger," and in *The Book of Los* (1795, K. 260) he forges the sun with them.

> 5. Roaring indignant, the bright sparks
> Endur'd the vast Hammer; but unwearied
> Los beat on the Anvil, till glorious
> An immense Orb of fire he fram'd.

> 6. Oft he quench'd it beneath in the Deeps,
> Then survey'd the all bright mass, Again
> Siezing fires from the terrific Orbs,
> He heated the round Globe, then beat,
> While, roaring, his Furnaces endur'd
> The chain'd Orb in their infinite wombs.[55]

The furnace in which the energy-symbols of Sun and Tyger are created is the prophetic imagination: the Hammer is the divine Word. The meanings of these images are supported by, though they do not depend on, their use in the Bible, Paracelsus, and Boehme. In Ezekiel xxii.17-22, the furnace is a simile for the wrath of God:

> And the word of the LORD came unto me, saying,
> Son of man, the house of Israel is to me become dross: all they are brass, and tin, and iron, and lead, in the midst of the furnace; they are even the dross of silver.

> Therefore thus saith the Lord GOD; Because ye are all become dross, behold, therefore I will gather you into the midst of Jerusalem.

> As they gather silver, and brass, and iron, and lead, and tin, into the midst of the furnace, to blow the fire upon it, to melt it; so will I

---

[54] As noted by Hazard Adams, *Blake and Yeats: The Contrary Vision* (Ithaca, N.Y.), p. 238.

[55] This similarity is discussed in my Brown Univ. master's thesis, "William Blake's Revolutionary Symbolism" (1957), p. 7, and in Miner, " 'The Tyger'," pp. 67-68.

gather you in mine anger and in my fury, and I will leave you there, and melt you.

Yes, I will gather you, and blow upon you in the fire of my wrath, and ye shall be melted in the midst thereof.

As silver is melted in the midst of the furnace, so shall ye be melted in the midst thereof; and ye shall know that I the LORD have poured out my fury upon you.

But the furnace does more than melt down; it also purifies: "Behold, I have refined thee, but not with silver; I have chosen thee in the furnace of affliction" (Isaiah xlviii.10). The furnace can be creative as well as destructive, as we see in Psalm xii—"The words of the LORD; are pure words: as silver tried in a furnace of earth, purified seven times." The destructive fire of wrath is also the energy of purification. Paracelsus, who believes that destruction perfects that which is good, regards the work of the alchemist's furnace as analogous to this divine activity: "For in the same way as God created the heaven and the earth, the Furnace with its fire must be constructed and regulated." "But the sun receives light from no other source than God Himself, Who rules, it, so that in the sun God Himself is burning and shining. Just so it is with this Art. The fire in the furnace may be compared to the sun. It heats the furnace and the vessels, just as the sun heats the vast universe. For as nothing can be produced in the world without the sun, so . . . nothing can be produced without this simple fire."[56] Blake carries the alchemical analogy into symbolism—the imaginative activity of the poet-prophet in raising the perceptions of mankind is, metaphorically, the Great Work of turning base metals into gold. Blake's furnace is a perpetual source of power for transforming a dead world. The Hammer, the active force of the *Logos*, beats out the changes. "Is not my word as a fire? saith the LORD and like a hammer that breaketh the rock in pieces?" (Jeremiah xxv.29). Boehme speaks of the Spirit of God as "the right Hammer" which strikes in the soul and makes it long for the love of God. "Such a soul is *easy* to be awakened . . . especially when the Hammer of the Holy Ghost sounds through the Ears into the Heart, then the tincture of the soul receives it *instantly;* and there it goes forth through the /551/ whole soul."[57] As if in answer to the closing questions of "The Tyger," in *Jerusalem*, plate 73, all

---

56 "Concerning the Spirits of the Planets," *The Hermetic and Alchemical Writings of Paracelsus*, ed. A. E. Waite (London, 1894), I, 85, 74.

57 *The Threefold Life of Man*, 1849, p. 194.

things are created in Los's furnaces, including "the tyger" and "the wooly lamb" (K. 713); and in *The Book of Los*, after creating the sun, "Los smiled with joy" (K. 260).

I do not suggest that we must literally find answers to the questions of Blake's poem in his sources or in his other writings. What these materials can do is reinforce and corroborate our sense of what the poem means; they also indicate the place of "The Tyger" in Blake's thought. Here the significance of Los as creator is especially important: the Tyger is, to adapt Coleridge's phrase, an educt of the prophetic imagination. Incarnating divine Wrath, it calls to mind the Prophets' representations of God as a beast of prey, the Greyhound of Virgil's prophecy in Canto i of the *Inferno,* and the Lion of the tribe of Juda in Revelation v.5.[58] Its fearful symmetry derives from the dialectical tension of Boehme's First and Second Principles. It inaugurates a Day of Wrath in which man will be tried by fire, but its ultimate function is to create a world in which Innocence will be possible. Those who follow vision through the fallen world of Experience, like the parents of "The Little Girl Found," will discover this.

> Then they followed
> Where the vision led,
> And saw their sleeping child
> Among tygers wild.

How this can be, how (not whether) the Tyger of Wrath can have the same origin as the Lamb of Love, is what Blake's poem asks. The "answer" does not lie with the horses of instruction who vindicate the ways of God to man. Through its imagery and language, with their traditional associations, "The Tyger" leads the responsive reader to an experience of the sublime.

---

[58] Cf. the "Christ the tiger" of Eliot's "Gerontion," in which several other lines also recall Blake:

> Virtues
> Are forced upon us by our impudent crimes.
> These tears are shaken from the wrath-bearing tree.

> The tiger springs in the new year. Us he devours.

Rodney M. Baine

Blake's "Tyger":
The Nature of the Beast*

The fascinated vision of William Blake's "Tyger" has probably always been basically clear to the uninitiate as well as to the adept in poetry. But concerning the symbolism of the Tyger, learning and ingenuity have lately taxed themselves to offer increasingly subtle and extravagant suggestions, so extravagant that Northrop Frye has remarked in connection with the poem "how often the popular estimate of Blake is sounder in perspective than the scholarly one."[1] This paper will not incorporate and attempt to refute the interpretations of those who view Blake's Tyger as Christ militant or energy or revelation or imaginative thought or transhuman values.[2] But a reading of "The Tyger" in the context of *Songs of Innocence and of Experience* and of its analogues or sources reveals it as the shocked and fascinated reaction of an observer imaginatively visualizing the creation of brutal cruelty in nature and in man, as symbolized by the Tyger. For the understanding of the poem several sources help: the engraved poem itself

* Reprinted from *Philological Quarterly*, XLVI (October, 1967), 488-498, by permission of The University of Iowa Department of Publications.

[1] Northrop Frye, *Fables of Identity: Studies in Poetic Mythology* (New York, 1963), p. 140. To the suggestions of Mr. Frye and of Mr. John E. Grant, who have read this paper, the writer is deeply indebted. Neither scholar, of course, subscribes completely to the views here stated.

[2] A convenient, annotated bibliography of interpretations of "The Tyger" is furnished by Hazard Adams in his *William Blake: a Reading of the Shorter Poems* (University of Washington Press, 1963), pp. 329-32. A survey of some critical positions is provided in Philip Hobsbaum's "A Rhetorical Question Answered: Blake's Tyger and its Critics," *Neophilologus*, XLVIII (1964), 151-155. Among the most interesting studies of the language is Fred Robinson's "Verb Tenses in Blake's 'The Tyger,' " *PMLA*, LXXIX (1964), 666-669. The December 1966 issue of *PMLA* contains a criticism of this article and a rejoinder, both by Mr. John E. Grant, and a reply and a surrejoinder by Mr. Robinson.

primarily and its preliminary drafts; other lyrics in *Songs of Innocence* and *Songs of Experience;* and the sources or analogues of the tiger symbol.

In the engraved poem two aspects of the creature are unmistakably clear: its symmetry and its horror. It is "burning bright," and twice its "symmetry" is pointed out. Pictorially considered, the Tyger is "burning bright" because its yellow stripes perhaps catch some gleams of light and, more obviously, because its luminous /489/ eyes provide a brilliant contrast to the surrounding night. About this same time, Blake in his *Vision of the Daughters of Albion* (1793) visualized "the glowing tyger."[3] Since Blake and his London readers had seen cats and perhaps even tigers enough, this realistic aspect of the Tyger demands no literary source.[4] But in his *Theron and Aspasio* (1755), to which Steelyard mistakenly refers in *An Island in the Moon,* James Hervey had pictured, "Amidst the inaccessible Depths of the Forest" how "the fiery Tyger springs upon his Prey." Then in his *History of the Earth and Animated Nature* (1774), Oliver Goldsmith, borrowing from Buffon, had commented on this practical feature of the feline eye: "In the eyes of cats . . . this contraction and dilation of the pupil, is so considerable, that the pupil, which by day-light appears narrow and small like the black of one's nail, by night expands over the whole surface of the eye-ball, and, as every one must have seen, their eyes seem on fire . . . the animal is thus better adapted for spying out and surprising its prey."[5]

Concerning this feature of his Tyger Blake was specific in his drafts of the poem preserved in the Rossetti Manuscript, where he clearly implied in the gleam the cruelty and fury of the Tyger—in "The cruel fire of thine eye" and "thy eyes of fury."[6] Though the gleam from this Avenue into Eternity may to some extent symbolize the potentially redemptive spark in an otherwise imbruted creature, it no more assures redemptive force than do the various fires flickering in the murky depths of Dante's Inferno or

---

[3] *The Complete Writings of William Blake,* ed. Geoffrey Keynes (London, 1957), p. 195. Except for those from "The Tyger" and *The Four Zoas* all subsequent citations from Blake will be taken from this edition, designated as K, and incorporated in the text.

[4] The tigers which could have been seen by Blake and contemporary Londoners are discussed in Paul Miner's " 'The Tyger': Genesis and Evolution in the Poetry of William Blake," *Criticism,* IV (1962), 59-73.

[5] James Hervey, *Theron and Aspasio, or a Series of Dialogues and Letters upon the most Important and Interesting Subjects* (London, 1755), III, 14, 15. Oliver Goldsmith, *A History of the Earth, and Animated Nature,* 2d. ed. (London, 1789), III, 205-06. Subsequent quotations from Goldsmith will cite this edition and be incorporated in the text.

[6] Readings from the Rossetti Manuscript are based upon the reproductions of pp. 108 and 109 in *The Note-Book of William Blake Called the Rossetti Manuscript,* ed. Geoffrey Keynes (London, 1935).

the fires without light in Milton's Hell.[7] More obviously, the symbolism of /490/ the gleam suggests damnation rather than salvation. Here the story of the naive freshman who thought Blake's Tyger on fire is more apt than amusing: the Tyger is not a source of light in himself, but is on fire, raging from his own malice and symbolizing the wrath of nature red in tooth and claw and of raging, fallen man. Somewhat of this symbolic use of fire appears in the contemporary *First Book of Urizen:*

> All the seven deadly sins of the soul
> In living creations appear'd,
> In the flames of eternal fury.
>
> . . . . .
> But no light from the fires: all was darkness
> In the flames of Eternal fury. (K, p. 225)

The naturalist Buffon had already commented upon the tiger's unslakable thirst for blood as a raging fever: "as blood only augments their thirst, they have often occasion for water, to cool the fervour which consumes them."[8] But the symbolism is particularly clear in Jacob Boehme, who evidently influenced Blake at this time. In *The Treatise of the Incarnation* Boehme divided the two principles, the light-flaming or holy property, from the "fierce *wrath* in the Fire." "The Fire is called *Nature;* the Light is not called Nature: it has indeed the fire's property; but it *changes it* out of fierce wrath into Love, out of devouring consuming, into generating, out of enmity and hatred, and bitter woe and torment, into meek well-doing, pleasant amiable desiring, and a perpetual satisfying and fulfilling."[9]

No more favorable symbolism for the nature of the Tyger than the gleam is the "fearful symmetry." The Tyger as an embodiment of the sublime Blake found in an aesthetic treatise which he read in his youth and remembered clearly even if he did not admire—Edmund Burke's *Philosophical Inquiry into the Origin of our Ideas of the Sublime and*

---

[7] Dante's fires of Hell are compared with the Tyger's fire by John E. Grant in his perceptive and comprehensive study "The Art and Argument of 'The Tyger,' " *Discussions of William Blake,* ed. John E. Grant (Boston, 1961), p. 71. Mr. Grant has privately pointed out Spenser's use of the phrase "burning bright" in a demonic context for the description of a furnace (*FQ,* II, vii, 35, 5).

[8] Georges Louis Le Clerc, Count de Buffon, *Natural History, General and Particular,* ed. William Smellie, 2d. ed. (London, 1785), V, 155. In his *Philosophy of Natural History* (Edinburgh, 1790), Smellie summarized the materials of Buffon and Goldsmith concerning the tiger (pp. 378-79).

[9] *The Works of Jacob Behmen, the Teutonic Theosopher* (London, 1764-81), II, 19, 37. All subsequent quotations from Behmen will be taken from this edition and incorporated in the text.

Beautiful (1757). Burke selected the tiger as an exhibit of the sublime because he is not only strong but "pernicious": "the sublime . . . comes upon us in the gloomy forest, and in the howling wilderness, in the form of the lion, the tiger, the panther."[10] Although Buffon had commented upon the dispropor- /491/ tion of the tiger,[11] Goldsmith omitted these details and emphasized instead the irony of its "fearful symmetry": " THE ancients had a saying, *That as the peacock is the most beautiful among birds, so is the tiger among quadrupedes.* In fact, no quadrupede can be more beautiful than this animal; the glossy smoothness of his hair, which . . . shines with greater brightness, than even that of the leopard; the extreme blackness of the streaks with which he is marked, and the bright yellow colour of the ground which they diversify, at once strike the beholder. To this beauty of colouring is added an extremely elegant form. . . . Unhappily, however, this animal's disposition is as mischievous as its form is admirable, as if Providence was willing to shew the small value of beauty, by bestowing it on the most noxious of quadrupedes' " (III, 233-34).

But more important than the Tyger's "fearful symmetry" is its "deadly terrors." Obviously it must be preternaturally horrible rather than superbly splendid if for its creation the questioner must imagine a fearsome and dreadful creator. More detail concerning this fearful nature of the Tyger exists in the Rossetti Manuscript, where the questioner exhibits the cruelty and fury of the Tyger in "The cruel fire of thine eye" and asks

> What dread hand & what dread feet
> Could fetch it from the furnace deep
> And in thy horrid ribs dare steep
> In the well of sanguine woe
> In what clay & in what mould
> Were thy eyes of fury rolld

The details "horrid ribs," the "eyes of fury," and the "well of sanguine woe" leave no doubt that the Tyger was conceived not as a splendid creature but a fascinating and horrible emblem of death and destruction.[12]

---

[10] *A Philosophical Enquiry into the Origin of our Ideas of the Sublime and Beautiful,* 3d. ed. (London, 1761), p. 114.

[11] Buffon, V, 155.

[12] In his "Blake's Revisions of *The Tyger*," in *PMLA*, LXXI (1956), 669-85, Mr. Martin Nurmi has suggested that Blake twice during the space of a few weeks, or days, in 1792/1793 revised his poem as he changed his mind about the implications of the Tyger—as he became more pessimistic or optimistic according to the pattern of events then unfolding in France. Blake surely agreed with his Harper in the *Marriage of Heaven and Hell:* "The man who never alters his opinion is like standing water, & breeds reptiles of the mind" (*K*, p. 156). Concerning the problem of the origin of evil, moreover, it is

Probably for this reason Blake rejected the /492/ penultimate line above: clay and mould suggest a yielding, fruitful softness and pliability in the creature inconsistent with the hardness of the Tyger. Elsewhere in the *Songs,* moreover, the clod of clay is used to symbolize unselfish, life-giving qualities.

Although the drafts of "The Tyger" furnish perhaps the clearest commentary on the nature of the creature, other poems from *Songs of Innocence* and *Songs of Experience* provide the context within which Blake intended that the poem should be read and understood. The nature of the Tyger cannot be fully understood apart from the nature of the Lamb, its antithesis; and Blake made sure that the reader would understand the contrast by having his questioner in "The Tyger" ask pointedly, "Did he who made the Lamb make thee?" The nature of the Lamb is clear: it has "clothing of delight," clothing which it shares with others. It brings happiness and joy instead of the terror of the Tyger. Its nature is further revealed by its identification with the child and with the Lamb of God:

> He is called by thy name
> For he calls himself a lamb.
> He is meek, & he is mild;
> He became a little child.
> I a child, & thou a lamb,
> We are called by his name.
>   (K, p. 115)

In "Night" it is by the Lamb of God that the nocence or noxiousness of the Tyger can be changed into innocence, so that

> "Wrath, by his meekness,
> "And by his health, sickness
> "Is driven away
> "From our immortal day."
>   (K, p. 119)

Thus the Tyger is more than a symbol of ferocity or cruelty in external nature. Although there is nothing in "The Tyger" to identify tigerish rapacity and cruelty with human, an analogous suggestion appears in "The

---

perhaps most difficult of all to determine. But to assume that Blake's ethical and religious ideas were at the mercy of developments in France and to read poetical revisions in the light of this assumption has already been demonstrated dangerous even for such a prolonged work as *The Four Zoas.* There is no cogent evidence to show that Blake's revisions in "The Tyger" were anything but the sensitive and perceptive strengthening of the poem as by selecting apter imagery and repressing adjectives and some details, the poet made his Tyger more shocking, more mysterious, more effective.

Lamb." The subtitle of *Songs of Innocence and of Experience,* moreover,
announces the two sets of poems as "Shewing the Two Contrary States of
the Human Soul" (K, p. 210). Thus "The Divine Image" of *Songs of
Innocence* exhibits unfallen, or redeemed man. The contrary state of the
human soul, "A Divine Image," etched about 1794 for *Songs of
Experience,* though never included there, exhibits fallen man as noxious
beast, in a state of nature:

> Cruelty has a Human Heart,
> And Jealousy a Human Face;
> Terror the Human Form Divine,
> And Secrecy the Human Dress.   /493/
>
> The Human Dress is forged Iron,
> The Human Form a fiery Forge,
> The Human Face a Furnace seal'd,
> The Human Heart its hungry Gorge. (K, p. 221)

The cruelty in natural or fallen man is the same cruelty and voracity
embodied in the Tyger; and the very phrases—"forged Iron," "fiery Forge,"
"a Furnace,"—recall the forging of the Tyger. Thus the creation of the
Tyger is not only the appearance of terror in external nature, but the
imbrutation of man himself.

But far more helpful for the interpretation of "The Tyger" than Blake's
later poems are the traditional symbols which were common to the heritage
of both poet and contemporary reader. Had Blake not intended the Lamb
and the Tyger to symbolize unfallen or redeemed man and fallen or
imbruted man, he would have chosen other, unambiguous symbols.
Although Mr. S. Foster Damon, Miss Kathleen Raine, and others have made
a beginning here, the sources and analogues of Blake's Tyger symbol have
not been adequately investigated.[13] From classical literature to Blake's own
day, the tiger had been singled out to symbolize natural ferocity and
cruelty, as for example in Medea, the tigress whose jealous revenge drives
her to slay her own young. The tradition is perhaps best exemplified in
Shakespeare, whose artistry and symbolism undoubtedly exercised a strong
influence upon Blake. In Shakespeare the tiger appears almost invariably as
the symbol of cruelty or inhuman savagery. When Coriolanus is thought to
be unrelenting toward Rome, Agrippa says of him, "There is no more
mercy in him, than there is milk in a male tyger" (V, iv, 30-31).[14] In

---

[13] S. Foster Damon, *William Blake: his Philosophy and Symbols* (New York,
1947), pp. 276-79; Kathleen Raine, "Blake's Debt to Antiquity," *Sewanee Review,*
LXXI (1963), 424-36, and "Who Made the Tyger!" *Encounter,* II (1954), 43-50. At
the time of writing, Miss Raine's promised *Blake and Traditional Mythology* had not
appeared. Mr. Coleman O. Parsons' "Tygers Before Blake" also awaits publication.

Henry VI, Part III the Duke of York accuses the "she-wolf of France," Queen Margaret:

> Oh, tygres heart wrapp'd in a woman's hide!

> But you are more inhuman, more inexorable,—
> O, ten times more,—than tygers of Hyrcania (I, iv, 137;
>   VI, 453, 455)

But perhaps the most memorable such characterization occurs in /494/ *King Lear,* where the shocked Albany, addressing Goneril and Regan, links tiger and Leviathan:

> Tygers, not daughters, what have you perform'd?

> If that the heavens do not their visible spirits
> Send quickly down to tame these vile offenses,
> 'Twil come, humanity must perforce prey on
> Itself, like
> Monsters of the deep. (IV, ii, 40; IX, 504)

That Blake remembered this passage seems clear from his *Tiriel* (ca. 1789), where the aged hero twice addresses his sons as "Serpents, not sons" (K, pp. 99, 105).

Milton could have contributed to the tiger symbolism, for in *Paradise Lost* Satan becomes briefly a tiger; but the animal symbolism is fully developed in Jacob Boehme and Emanuel Swedenborg. Boehme used the wild animal to symbolize evil in fallen man. Perhaps his clearest explanation of these spiritual correspondences he embodied in his *Mysterium Magnum:*

> Here the Craft and Subtlety of the Serpent was manifest, and the precious Image was corrupted, and became according to the *Limus* of the Earth a *Beast* of all Beasts: Whereupon there are now so many and varied Properties in Man; as one a Fox, Wolf, Bear, Lion . . . and, in brief, as many Kinds of Creatures as are upon the Earth, so many and *various* Properties likewise there are in the earthly Man . . . .

---

14 *The Plays of William Shakespeare,* ed. Samuel Johnson and George Steevens, 2d. ed. (London, 1778), VII, 491. All subsequent references will quote this edition and be incorporated in the text, citing volume and page. Given first will be act, scene, and line numbers taken from *The Complete Works of Shakespeare,* ed. George Lyman Kittredge (Boston, 1936).

Not that the whole Man is such a [very brute Beast in outward shape,] but there is such a *Figure* of the Desire in the earthly Essence; and the Man must bear *such* a Beast in the Body, which stirs him up and drives him to the bestial Property; *not* that he has this Form according to the outward [Person,] but *really* in the earthly Essence . . . .

Yet this Beast does somewhat put forth its *Signature* externally in every one; if one does but observe and well mind the same, he may find it: Hence Christ called the Pharisees *a Generation of Vipers, and the Seed of Serpents;* also others he called *Wolves, ravening Wolves* . . . and the like, for they were such in their earthly Essence: And he taught us, *that we must be born anew*, and forsake this bestial Property, *and become as Children, or we should not possess the Kingdom of God.*

The contrary state of the Lamb, Boehme clarified in his *Of the Election of Graces:* "The like is to be understood concerning the tame good Beasts; that many a Man is in the Property of the kind or *good Beast*" (III, 86; IV, 202).

Although in his *Marriage of Heaven and Hell* (1793) Blake severely criticized some aspects of the system of Swedenborg, particularly his apparent predestinarianism, about the time that Blake evolved his plan for the contraries of the Lamb and the Tyger he was apparently attracted by other aspects of Swedenborgianism. At any rate, in April of 1789 he and "C. Blake," probably his wife, Catherine, attended in London a five-day general conference on the doctrines of the Master and subscribed an affirmation which ap- /495/ proved the establishment of the New Jerusalem Church.[15] His symbolism Blake probably owed in part to Swedenborg who, following Boehme, developed a system of "the correspondence of spiritual things with natural." "The animals of the earth in general correspond to affections," Swedenborg explained; "the gentle and useful ones, to good affections, the savage and useless, to evil affections. In particular, . . . sheep and lambs [correspond], to the affections of the spiritual mind. . . . Man, too, is similar to animals as to his natural man, and therefore is compared to them in common discourse. If he be of a gentle disposition, he is called a sheep or a lamb; if of a savage temper, he is called a bear or a wolf. . . ." Swedenborg maintained that this symbolic

---

[15] Charles Higham, "Blake and the 'Swedenborgians,' " *Notes and Queries*, 11th Ser., XI (10 April 1915), 276. Mr. David V. Erdman reminds us that Blake's attendance only on 13 April is certain: "Blake's Early Swedenborgianism: A Twentieth-Century Legend," *Comparative Literature*, V (1953), 253.

system was not merely conventional: in angelic discourse "such things fall into representative species of animals; when the discourse is concerning good affections, there are exhibited beautiful, tame, and useful animals . . . as lambs, sheep. . . . But the discourse of the angels concerning evil affections is represented by beasts of a terrible appearance, fierce, and useless, as by tigers, bears, wolves, scorpions, serpents. . . . "16

Blake must have been influenced not only by this system of natural correspondences, but by Buffon's and Goldsmith's selection of the tiger as the most cruel and bloodthirsty of all the wild animals. According to the natural historians, its malignity is proverbial. Paraphrasing Buffon, Goldsmith suggested that it is "fierce without provocation, and cruel without necessity." "In falling in among a flock or an herd, it gives no quarter, but levels all with indiscriminate cruelty, and scarce finds time to appease its appetite, while intent upon satisfying the malignity of its nature." Alone among wild animals, Goldsmith added, it is untamable: "The /496/ caresses of the keeper have no influence on their heart of iron; and time, instead of mollifying its disposition, only serves to encrease its fierceness and malignity" (III, 235, 238).

In developing his Tyger symbol, Blake was probably influenced not only by the naturalists but by the physiognomists. In his *Essays on Physiognomy*, J. C. Lavater, whose *Aphorisms* (1788 or early 1789) Blake annotated, set the theme of "The Tyger": "What bloodthirsty cruelty, what insidious craft in the eye, and snout, of the tiger! Can the laugh of Satan himself, at a falling saint, be more fiendlike than the head of a triumphant tiger?" Lavater went on to remark upon the delight which the tiger, like the cat, finds in tormenting its victim: "Unmerciful to birds and mice as the tiger to the lamb. They delight in prolonging torture before they devour. . . ."17 Blake may well have had these passages in mind, as

16Emanuel Swedenborg, *Heaven and its Wonders and Hell, from Things Heard and Seen* (Philadelphia, 1885), par. 110, pp. 71, 71-72; *Arcana Coelestia: the Heavenly Arcana contained in the Holy Scripture of the Word of the Lord Unfolded . . . together with Wonderful Things Seen in the World of Spirits and in the Heaven of Angels* (New York, 1870-74), par. 3218, III, 424. By 1788 three volumes of the *Arcana Coelestia*, as well as *Heaven and its Wonders*, had been published in an English translation. This idea of spiritual correspondence is so frequently reiterated in Swedenborg that even a temporary Swedenborgian like Blake could hardly have missed it. For other examples see *The True Christian Religion*, 2d. ed. (London, 1786), par. 45, p. 66; par. 312, p. 291; and *Arcana Coelestia*, par. 45, I, 21. Paul Miner cited (p. 60) Swedenborg's *Heaven and Hell*, par. 388, and suggested that Blake had paraphrased *The True Christian Religion*, par. 388, in his *Marriage of Heaven and Hell*, K., pp. 155, 157.

17 J. C. Lavater, *Essays on Physiognomy, for the Promotion of the Knowledge and the Love of Mankind*, trans. Thomas Holcroft (London, 1789), II, 170. Since Lavater approved the translation and the accompanying plates of this volume on 9 June 1784, and made additions printed on a separate sheet (Y), this evidence, along with the blank page (X[8]verso), following the close of the text proper, would suggest that Lavater read the printed sheets. Since Blake was engraving for Holcroft in *The Wit's Magazine* in

well as *Hamlet* and Goldsmith, when at the end of his *Island in the Moon* Quid, an amateur in physiognomy, asks Miss Gittipin, or Mrs. Nannicantipot:

"Don't you think I have something of the Goat's face?" says he.
"Very like a Goat's face," she answer'd.
"I think your face," said he, "is like that noble beast the Tyger."
(K, p. 62)

The irony of the compliment would have been especially apparent to anyone familiar with Lavater. So would the ironies implicit in the earlier scene where Mrs. Gimblet, listening to the Antiquarian Etruscan Column discourse concerning "virtuous cats" "was thinking of the shape of her eyes and mouth" (K, p. 44). Probably Lavater's emphasis upon the teeth of the crocodile (Leviathan) and the eyes and snout of the tiger and the general practice among physiognomists and natural historians to avoid prominent display of the tiger's fangs in their illustrations led Blake to engrave a tiger inadequately ferocious to satisfy some of his commentators.[18] In the quite similar head of the tiger engraved in Holcroft's translation of Lavater the mouth is closed (facing II, 171). "The fiery, /497/ sharp-angled, eyes," Lavater suggested, ignoring the teeth completely, "the broad flat nose, or rather what is analogous to the nose, and, especially, the line of the mouth, all betoken the fearfully brutal and the cruel" (II, 172). Swedenborg also had pointed out the symbolic importance of the snout: "The natural Man, who is become sensual by Evils and consequent Falses, in the spiritual World in the Light of Heaven does not appear as a Man, but as a Monster, also with a Nose retracted . . ., because the Nose corresponds to the Perception of Truth: He also cannot bear a Ray of heavenly Light, but what is like that of a Coal-fire."[19] Such suggestions Blake may well have remembered also in Tirzah's and Erin's account of the embodiment of man in *The Four Zoas* and *Jerusalem:*

These nostrils that Expanded with delight in morning skies
I have bent downward with lead molten in my roaring furnaces.[20]

1784, this version, probably already printed, was easily accessible to him even before the early dates suggested for *An Island in the Moon.*

[18] In his *Blake: Prophet against Empire* (Princeton University Press, 1954), for example, Mr. David Erdman complains that "his tiger is not even baring his fangs" (p. 180, n. 33).

[19] Swedenborg, *The Wisdom of the Angels concerning Divine Love and Divine Wisdom* (London, 1788), p. 216.

[20] *Vala or The Four Zoas*, ed. G. E. Bentley, Jr. (Oxford: Clarendon Press, 1963), p. 111. A subsequent reference, embodied in the text, will cite this edition as FZ.

"The Nostrils, bent down to the earth & clos'd with senseless flesh
"That odours cannot them expand, nor joy on them exult: . . ."
                                                        (K, p. 680)

Perhaps the clearest commentary on what Blake intended his Tyger and
his Lamb to symbolize came, a few years after the *Songs* were engraved,
from his friend Henry Fuseli, with whom Blake had worked closely in the
late 1780's to provide plates for Henry Hunter's translation of Lavater's
Physiognomy. Writing an Advertisement for the now completed edition,
Fuseli commented: "Were man and man as easily discriminated as the lamb
and the tiger, the Physiognomist's would be a useless science; but since
both lamb and tiger may dwell in human frames, he surely deserved our
thanks, who points them out to us before we wound the one or sink
beneath the other."[21] According to Fuseli, then, Blake's use of the
contraries of the Tyger and the Lamb is similar to that of the Spectre and
Urthona in *The Four Zoas*. There the Tyger surrogate, "a ravening
hungering & thirsting cruel lust & murder," warns Urthona, /498/

Thou knowest that the Spectre is in Every Man insane brutish
Deformed that I am thus a ravening devouring lust. . . .
                                                    (FZ, pp. 87, 86)

Perhaps Blake's clearest explanation is found in "To the Deists," in his
Jerusalem: "Man is born a Spectre or Satan & is altogether an Evil, &
requires a New Selfhood continually, & must continually be changed into
his direct Contrary" (K, p. 682).

---

21 John Caspar Lavater, *Essays on Physiognomy, designed to Promote the
Knowledge and the Love of Mankind*, trans. Henry Hunter (London, 1789-98), I, Sig. A
[2] recto. This inserted Advertisement does not form part of the original Volume I but
was probably written shortly before Hunter's Preface, which is dated 24 December 1798.
Fuseli's Advertisement, including the complete passage quoted here, was reprinted
virtually intact in *The Monthly Review*, Ser. 2, XXXIV (1801), 12-16.

Kay Parkhurst Long

William Blake and
the Smiling Tyger*

William Blake's "The Tyger" is, in many ways, an example of verbal nonsense literature, a literary genre today most frequently connected with Lewis Carroll and Edward Lear, but also evident at times in such diverse authors as Rabelais, Samuel Johnson, John Keats, John Milton, and Christina Rossetti.[1] "The Tyger" may be unmistakably, and most importantly, identified with this literature as it shares the *raison d'être* of the nonsensical—a rhetoric of indirection.

Sigmund Freud, in his study of the sources of the comic, traces the delight in nonsense to the feeling of freedom we encounter when we are able to abandon the pressures of logic.[2] The authors of verbal nonsense abandon the logic of language for the freedom of the nonsensical extreme. They stress indirectly that human logic is a barrier to human freedom. In the whimsical humor of their writings, they enumerate the various guises of restrictive human logic—they parody the tragic nonsense of these man-created restrictions through nonsense. Perhaps their rhetoric of indirection is simply understood in that cliched solution to any tragic situation: if you laugh at the tragedy, it will go away. The nonsense

---

* This article was written especially for this volume. Quotations and paraphrases from the article can be documented by citing the page numbers in this casebook.

[1] Martin Esslin in *The Theatre of the Absurd* (New York, 1961), p. 241, calls Rabelais one of the greatest masters of nonsense prose and verse. The nonsense prose of Rabelais is evidenced by *Gargantua* and *Pantagruel.* Samuel Johnson's *Rasselas* has many affinities with nonsense prose. Some of John Keats' uncollected poems, derived from his letters, belong to the nonsense genre. See under the heading "Trivia" in *The Poetical Works*, ed. H. W. Garrod (Oxford, 1958), pp. 554-569. John Milton's "On the Oxford Carrier" is frequently cited as a nonsense poem. Christina Rossetti has many poems of this type. See *The Poetical Works*, Memoir and Notes by William Michael Rossetti (London, 1928), pp. 417-446.

[2] "Wit and Its Relation to the Unconscious," *The Basic Writings of Sigmund Freud*, ed. and trans. A. A. Brill (New York, 1938), particularly pages 717-719.

115

authors hope that, as their readers laugh at the compulsions of humanity, they will become aware that such compulsions do exist, and that they then will do something to see that the compulsions go away.

In "The Tyger" William Blake parodies what he views as a major compulsion of mankind—the tendency to generalize, to label, to categorize.

To view completely in what way Blake's "The Tyger" is a kind of nonsense verse, we must recapture the experience of first reading the poem. We recall the magic of its rhythm, the appeal of its sound patterns. It was catchy, easy to repeat, much as a nursery rhyme. Yet, what did it mean? We were confused, but we didn't heed our confusion. We went back to the poem because it was memorable in its sounds and rhythms (the standards of nonsense verse). We admired Blake's tiger because he was present in a superb poem, regardless of what he was or who made him. This certainly was the single vision of innocence. But, with experience, we had to have another look at this tiger. So we began our attempt to label him, to put him into a niche in our scheme of things. And we distorted our vision until we fell into Blake's Bacon/Newton/Locke hell. We were using logic to restrict freedom.

Once we remember our first acquaintance with "The Tyger" and realize the impossibility of framing the poem or the animal into our standards of logic, we can combine the simplicity of innocent vision, with the broadened vision that can proceed from its contrary, experience, to enjoy and profit from William Blake's indirect rhetoric.[3]

Behind the speaker of "The Tyger" stands William Blake, laughing bitterly at his poetic character.[4] We, as readers, laugh too at the befuddled mind of this persona. The speaker is evidently trying to arrive at some formula for the tiger and for the world. He asks fourteen questions but he never reaches an answer for any of them. And his entire thinking process is injected with doubt, particularly reflected in the speaker's could / dare alternations. In "What immortal hand or eye / Could frame thy fearful

---

[3] Blake often evidences a tendency for the humorous. In the manuscript limericks, the inflated rhetoric of some of his letters, and especially in the illuminated engraving accompanying "The Tyger," he seems to delight in the comic. The drawing of the tiger appears to contrast sharply with the poem. A meek, clumsy, smiling tiger looks out on Blake's world. Geoffrey Keynes has noted that Blake has altered several of the drawings—so that there is no one tiger in Blake's pictorial art. Again, we seem to be confronted with a Blake communicating through the nonsensical.

[4] Raymond Lister in his recent book, *William Blake* (London, 1968), pp. 88-89 recognizes Blake's sense of humor. In discussing Blake's illustrations for Hayley's *Ballads* (1805), Lister points out that the silly pictures may "show us his sense of humour. The writer of *Songs of Innocence and of Experience* must have realized how hopelessly laughable the Hermit's verses were, and probably, with his tongue in his cheek, tried to give them equally laughable illustrations." Lister also cites Blake's account of a fairy's funeral as an example of Blake's straight-faced spoofing. Then, we might also see "The Tyger," both poem and illustration, as exhibiting this important aspect of Blake's writing and drawing: the nonsensical, the joking, the calculated put-on.

symmetry?" the speaker doubts that any deity would be able to create a tiger.[5] In "What immortal hand or eye / Dare frame thy fearful symmetry," the speaker doubts that any deity would have the courage to create a tiger. The oft-quoted line "Did he who made the Lamb make thee?" is injected with doubt that there is an immortal creator capable of superhuman accomplishments. The persona's doubt gets him nowhere, his questions lead him nowhere. We must laugh at the circular questioning process which ends with yet another question, and a question twin to the very first at that, except for one slight, and for that reason more humorous, change—"could" to "dare." The speaker of "The Tyger" is Blake's

> . . . idiot Questioner who is always questioning
> But never capable of answering, who sits with a sly grin
> Silent plotting when to question, like a thief in a cave,
> Who publishes doubt and calls it knowledge, whose Science is Despair.[6]

We next become aware that Blake's speaker is proceeding from an abstraction and is attempting to draw conclusions from it. In the first two lines of the poem he provides an abstract description of the tiger:

> Tyger! Tyger! burning bright
> In the forests of the night . . .

He says, evidently looking at a particular tiger, that this animal lives in a forest at nighttime and burns brightly. The literal meaning is hazy, and any symbolic interpretation is equally obscure. Fire, forest, and night all have double potentials for symbolic interpretation. We can't comprehend the generality. Can the speaker? The point remains that to Blake it is dangerous to theorize about any essence of the earth. He is elsewhere in his writings adamant about his stance on abstract reasoning:

> General Knowledge is Remote Knowledge; it is in Particulars that Wisdom consists and Happiness too.[7]

> To Generalize is to be an Idiot. To Particularize is the Alone Distinction of Merit. General Knowledges are those Knowledges that Idiots possess.[8]

---

[5] All quotations are from *Blake: Complete Writings*, ed. Geoffrey Keynes (London, 1966). "The Tyger," p. 214.

[6] "Milton," p. 533.

[7] "A Vision of the Last Judgment," p. 611.

[8] "Annotations to Reynolds," p. 451.

It is impossible to proceed from a general idea to knowledge. Such procedures of the mind result in an idiot questioner with circular questions. As Blake notes:

Knowledge is not by deduction, but Immediate by Perception or Sense at once.[9]

And the long process of questions with no answers surely indicates that the persona does not have immediate perception.

When we turn to the speaker's language we become trapped in a wryly humorous forest of ambiguities. The speaker first wonders "What immortal hand or eye" would be able to "frame" the tiger's "fearful symmetry." It must be remembered that Blake conceived of a god in man. He said that: "Human nature is the image of God,"[10] and that: "He who sees the Infinite in all things, sees God. He who sees the Ratio only, sees himself only."[11] If the speaker is drawing a line between the tiger and his "immortal" creator then he is seeing the ratio only. But if he is saying by his question, that there is actually no "immortal" being who would have been able to create ... We can't be certain, and apparently neither is the speaker.

The word "frame" is another instance that the speaker speaks in riddles. "Frame" may mean to shape or direct one's thoughts to; to shape the faculties or inclinations of; to make, construct, fashion, invent; to conceive. Each sense would impart a different meaning to the line. (Of course these meanings would be dependent on the reading of the preceding line.) Is there an immortal being capable of shaping the faculties or inclinations of the tiger—hence, restraining the tiger's might? Or perhaps, is there an immortal being capable of constructing such a marvelous creature? Or still, is there any immortal being capable of conceiving, apprehending, such a wondrous creature? The object of "frame" offers no illumination. "Fearful symmetry" can also have various interpretations. Does the speaker comply with Blake's notions of symmetry? If so, he would be afraid of symmetry because it was a characteristic admired by the rational thinkers of Blake's age. Blake connected symmetry and proportion with a mathematical approach to the universe, and to him God was "not a Mathematical Diagram."[12] He felt that:

9 "Annotations to Berkeley," p. 774.
10 "Annotations to Lavatar," p. 83.
11 "There is No Natural Religion," p. 98.
12 "Annotations to Berkeley," p. 774.

Harmony [and] Proportion are Qualities and Not Things. . . . Every
Thing has its own Harmony and Proportion, Two Inferior Qualities in
it. For its Reality is Its Imaginative Form.[13]

Demonstration Similitude and Harmony are Objects of Reasoning.
Invention, Identity and Melody are Objects of Intuition.[14]

But if the persona admired proportion, feeling that such form was
admirable, he would then be a proponent of mathematical diagrams. Do we
then consider "fearful symmetry" as his own perception of the tiger or as
his castigation of a rational world viewing its creatures as symmetrical? The
"ifs" are endless.

We can go through the poem, evidencing the confusing lines. All have
provoked numerous and varied commentaries. We must ask about the
"fire" of verse two, the last line. Is it the fire of the tiger's eyes? Another
classic confusion is the last line of stanza three: "What dread hand? and
What dread feet?" The hand we might identify with the creator, but what
about the feet? Next, we might approach the ambiguous pronoun "its" of
stanza four. But we tend to forget it as our eyes strike the first two lines
of verse five, perhaps the most controversial of all:

> When the stars threw down their spears,
> And water'd heaven with their tears . . .

These lines seem to belong to one of the prophecies, not to one of the
lyrics of experience. In fact, the first line is found almost in identical form
in *The Four Zoas*.[15] Significantly, these lines exist as the second of two
declarative statements in the poem. The other lines of declaration contain a
generalization. Are these, then, another abstraction? The speaker does
attempt deductions here also: "Did he smile his work to see? / Did he who
made the Lamb make thee?" Finally, should we deduce "yes" or "no" to
the questions of creation? We do not know, we cannot tell, for we are led
back to the beginning, with an ambiguous tiger burning brightly in
nighttime forests.

All we can be certain of now is that this intricate maze is humorous.
And, we are brought, in our laughter, to the instant perception that Blake's
speaker is humorous in his attempts to define the indefinable, to categorize

---

13 *Ibid.*

14 "Annotations to Reynolds," p. 474.

15 "The stars threw down their spears & fled naked away." *The Four Zoas.* p. 311.

what cannot or should not be categorized. This is the point of Blake's humorous indirection. This is the point of all nonsense literature. Through a kind of absurd laughter is communicated a clear awareness of existence.

William Blake has parodied a major compulsion of mankind. He views this compulsion, this mania for logic, as an indication of man's selfhood, hence a barrier to human freedom, which is obtained only by annihilation of selfhood.[16] Man tries to label and identify the essences of existence.[17] And Blake states:

> Essence is not Identity, but from Essence proceeds Identity and from one Essence may proceed many Identities . . .[18]

There is no one tiger, good or evil, but many tigers. The man who abstracts one tiger cannot see beyond his mundane shell to recognize the infinite variety of creation. He is an eighteenth-century chain-of-being philosopher. The man who would even ask "Did he who made the Lamb make thee?" has complied with the warning of Blake's axiom: "One Law for the Lion and Ox is Oppression."[19] He has shortsightedly overlooked that "creation is God descending according to the weakness of man, for our Lord is the word of God and everything on earth is the word of God and in its essence is God."[20] Consequently, such a man cannot see beyond the limits of his own individual logic—he cannot be free.

The variety of proposed meanings to "The Tyger" substantiates Blake's claim that man feels impelled to place all forms in their proper places. We hear variously of a good tiger, or a tiger of wrath, of a tiger from heaven, of a tiger from hell. We hear that he who created the lamb did create the tiger, that he who created the lamb couldn't possibly have created the tiger. Assuredly, just as Blake must have laughed when he created his tiger, he must now be laughing from his perspective in Jerusalem, arms clasped around a tiger, at the evidence of what man, in his penchant for restrictive logic, has created from his tiger. For to Blake, tiger, good or bad, from heaven or hell, kin or not kin to the lamb, was restriction. The vital importance was that a tiger, or any creature, exists as evidence of the unending potentials of the universe and of man's imaginative perceptions of

---

16 In "Milton," Keynes, p. 533, Blake says that "the Reasoning Power in Man . . . is a false Body, an Incrustation over . . . the Immortal / Spirit, a Selfhood which must be put off and annihilated alway."

17 This is the position of Bromion in "The Visions of the Daughters of Albion." See p. 192 in Keynes.

18 "Annotations to Swedenborg's Divine Love," p. 91.

19 "The Marriage of Heaven and Hell," p. 158.

20 "Annotations to Lavatar," p. 87.

the universe. To attempt to generalize, to categorize, to label that variety is to restrict freedom. This is the indirect rhetoric of nonsense literature from the smiling bard and his humorous beast.

Suggestions for Papers

Short Papers

"The Tyger" as an experience in sound and rhythm. Identify the uses made of alliteration, assonance, consonance, and rhyme; and identify the metrical structure of the poem. Dealing with the competence, pleasantness, significance of the sound and rhythm, make an evaluation of the poem as a sensory experience.

The use of metaphor in "The Tyger." Identify all the interior metaphors in the poem and evaluate their appropriateness. Discuss the relation of the interior metaphors to the metaphorical quality of the poem as a whole.

An interpretation of the line, "When the stars threw down their spears." Review the various interpretations given of this enigmatic line and then give your own interpretation.

The punctuation of "The Tyger." Discuss the importance of the punctuation in the poem, keeping in mind that some critics believe the meaning of the poem may be seriously impaired if proper punctuation is not achieved. Demonstrate in your paper how differing punctuations may lead to differing readings.

The significance of Blake's use of a tiger as symbol. Since the lion and the lamb are frequently used as dichotomous images of war and peace, violence and gentleness, rage and harmony, why is Blake's use of the tiger *instead of* the lion significant?

Blake's madness in "The Tyger." Blake's severest critics have called him mad. Using "The Tyger" as evidence, write an essay defending—or attacking—Blake's sanity. Is "The Tyger"—in your estimation—the product of a disturbed mind or an extremely rational mind?

"The Tyger" as an intellectually complicated poem. Defend or attack the thesis that the poem is highly "educated," requiring a great deal of study and explication before it can become meaningful to a reader.

The significance of "The Tyger" as a question poem. Discuss Blake's presentation of his poem as a set of questions. Do you feel the questions are "real"—that is, do you feel the poem is actually without any answers; or do you feel that the questions are used simply for rhetorical effect and that behind them Blake is actually making some sort of declaration and statement?

The nature of the tiger. Write a brief, rather simple report identifying Blake's "tyger" as an evil creature or as a good creature. Is the tiger really a symbol of evil and darkness or is the tiger a symbol of glory and power?

Long Papers

The significance of "The Tyger" as a poem with diverse meanings. Write an essay discussing the significance of the poem in the light of the various interpretations it has prompted. Do you feel that Blake's poem is in any way a failure because its meaning is not crystal clear? Or do you think the poem is successful because it does prompt a variety of different meanings?

The most acceptable reading of "The Tyger." Decide which essay or article in this casebook makes the most sense to you. Write your commentary, explaining why you feel the arguments in one particular article or essay appeal most to you and why you accept that particular interpretation of the poem.

Your own interpretation of "The Tyger." If you have an interpretation of "The Tyger" that you consider unique or at least different from any presented in this casebook, reveal that interpretation in a full-length essay.

Nineteenth-century reactions to "The Tyger." Write a paper dealing with some of the various nineteenth-century reactions referred to in the various articles and essays in this casebook. Can you piece together the general nineteenth-century attitude toward "The Tyger" and determine how that attitude differs from that of the twentieth century?

The critics of "The Tyger." Write a paper dealing with those critics and commentators who have disliked the poem in whole or in part. Is there some prevailing pattern of dislike? What theories of literature would seem to be operative in their criticism of the poem?

The development of interpretation of "The Tyger" in the twentieth century. The essays and articles in this casebook have been presented in chronological order—the original publication dates ranging from 1924 to 1969. Write a paper dealing with any developments or changes in attitude toward "The Tyger" over this forty-five year period.

Blake's religious position as revealed in "The Tyger." Write an essay in which you demonstrate that "The Tyger" is a religious poem and in which you explain what seems to be Blake's basic religious attitude in the poem.

Additional Readings

Bateson, F. W., ed. *Selected Poems of William Blake*. New York: Macmillan Company, 1957, pp. 117-119.

Bloom, Harold. *Blake's Apocalypse: A Study in Poetic Argument.* Garden City: Doubleday & Co., 1963, pp. 137-139.

Bowen, Robert O. "Blake's 'The Tyger,' 7-8," *Explicator*, VII (1949), item 62.

Bowra, C. M. *The Romantic Imagination.* Cambridge: Harvard University Press, 1949, pp. 47-49.

Erdman, David V. *Blake: Prophet Against Empire.* Princeton: Princeton University Press, 1954, pp. 178-181.

Gillham, D. G. *Blake's Contrary States: The 'Songs of Innocence and of Experience' as Dramatic Poems.* Cambridge: Cambridge University Press, 1966, pp. 243-248.

Gleckner, Robert F. *The Piper and the Bard.* Detroit: Wayne State University Press, 1959, pp. 277-287.

Grant, John E. "The Art and Argument of 'The Tyger,' " *Texas Studies in Literature and Language*, II (Spring, 1960), 38-60.

Grant, John E. and Fred C. Robinson, "Tense and the Sense of Blake's 'The Tyger,' " [An Exchange], *PMLA*, LXXXI (1966), 596-603.

Miner, Paul. " 'The Tyger': Genesis and Evolution in the Poetry of William Blake" *Criticism*, IV (1962), 59-73.

Ostriker, Alicia. *Vision and Verse in William Blake.* Madison: The University of Wisconsin Press, 1965, pp. 76-77, 86-88.

Raine, Kathleen. "Who Made the Tyger?" *Encounter*, II, No. 6 (June, 1954), 43-50.

Robinson, Fred C. "Verb Tense in Blake's 'The Tyger,' " *PMLA*, LXXIX (1964), 666-669.

Rudd, Margaret. *Divided Image.* London: Routledge and Kegan Paul, Ltd., 1953, pp. 87-91.

Sampson, John. *The Poetical Works of William Blake.* London: Oxford University Press, 1905, pp. 110-115.

Stone, George Winchester. "Blake's 'The Tyger,' " *Explicator,* I (1942), item 19.

Wicksteed, Joseph. *Blake's Innocence and Experience.* New York: E. P. Dutton, 1928, pp. 191-200.